Gospel-Shaped Marriage

Gospel-Shaped Marriage

Grace for Sinners to Love Like Saints

Chad Van Dixhoorn and
Emily Van Dixhoorn

Foreword by Alistair Begg

:: CROSSWAY®

WHEATON, ILLINOIS

Gospel-Shaped Marriage: Grace for Sinners to Love Like Saints

Copyright © 2022 by Chad Van Dixhoorn and Emily Van Dixhoorn

Published by Crossway
       1300 Crescent Street
       Wheaton, Illinois 60187

Cover design: Jordan Singer

First printing 2022

Printed in the United States of America

Trade paperback ISBN: 978-1-4335-8071-0
ePub ISBN: 978-1-4335-8074-1
PDF ISBN: 978-1-4335-8072-7
Mobipocket ISBN: 978-1-4335-8073-4

Library of Congress Cataloging-in-Publication Data

Names: Van Dixhoorn, Chad B., author. | Van Dixhoorn, Emily, author.
Title: Gospel-shaped marriage : grace for sinners to love like saints / Chad Van Dixhoorn and Emily
    Van Dixhoorn ; foreword by Alistair Begg.
Description: Wheaton, Illinois : Crossway, 2022. | Includes bibliographical references and indexes.
Identifiers: LCCN 2021046473 (print) | LCCN 2021046474 (ebook) | ISBN 9781433580710
    (hardcover) | ISBN 9781433580727 (pdf) | ISBN 9781433580734 (mobipocket) | ISBN
    9781433580741 (epub)
Subjects: LCSH: Marriage—Biblical teaching.
Classification: LCC BS680.M35 V36 2022 (print) | LCC BS680.M35 (ebook) | DDC 248.8/44—dc23
LC record available at https://lccn.loc.gov/2021046473
LC ebook record available at https://lccn.loc.gov/2021046474

Crossway is a publishing ministry of Good News Publishers.

LB		32	31	30	29	28	27	26	25	24	23	22
15	14	13	12	11	10	9	8	7	6	5	4	3	2

To all the singles and couples who made our marriage stronger,
and especially to Berta Badenoch, and Ian and Joan Hamilton

Contents

Foreword by Alistair Begg   *9*

Introduction   *13*

1   The Bible and Marriage   *15*

2   History and Marriage   *25*

3   Grace in Marriage   *37*

4   Women and Marriage   *47*

5   Men and Marriage   *63*

6   Winning in Marriage   *75*

7   Family and Marriage   *93*

8   Bedtime in Marriage   *107*

9   Growing in Marriage   *119*

Appendix: How to Change Your Spouse in Three
Easy Steps   *131*

Discussion Questions   *133*

Notes   *147*

General Index   *149*

Scripture Index   *153*

Foreword

ONE OF THE GREAT JOYS of pastoral ministry is found in the "solemnization of matrimony." It is a special privilege to be granted a ringside seat as one man and one woman enter this honorable estate instituted by God. There is benefit in using the archaic language of the *Book of Common Prayer* to remind us that marriage is not to be entered upon lightly or carelessly but thoughtfully, with reverence for God and with due consideration of the purposes for which it was established by God. Alongside procreation there is the preservation of human society, which can be strong and happy only where the marriage bond is held in honor. It is not uncommon when these words are read for the reaction to be an uneasy rapt silence or an uncomfortable restlessness in the congregation, because they challenge contemporary perspectives on the subject.

We are living through what is arguably the most rapid change in family structure in human history. The sexual revolution of the sixties, which held out hope for "true love" beyond the boundaries of God's perfect plan, has left in its wake moral, emotional, and social confusion. Families that function together and that do so with a shared set of moral values are increasingly an endangered species. Sociologists recognize that only a minority of American households are two-parent, mom-and-dad families. Marriage, where it is adopted, is no longer about childbearing or child-rearing but about personal fulfillment. Consider the falling birth rate and the fact that there are more American homes with pets than children! Our smartphones have made it possible for us to be "alone together." The decentralization of family life is accompanied by a fascination with genealogy—the quest is to find our roots and assure ourselves that we belong somehow, genetically, emotionally, mystically, and spiritually in a solidarity of souls.

Instead of denouncing the darkness, which is easy to do, the social climate presents us with an opportunity to shine as lights in the world. This means viewing marriage in the context of the gospel. The apostle Paul's specific directions for the Christian family are set within the larger framework of its place in the church family. He addresses his readers as "God's chosen ones" (Col. 3:12), part of a vast company of men and women throughout the ages who were sought out by God, heard the gospel, and understood the grace of God in truth. At the time of writing, directives for household management were common, but Paul is not simply providing a list of ethical demands; rather, he encourages his readers with the reminder that in Christ we are enabled to fulfill our assigned roles. The one-flesh union as established from the beginning is not based on fluctuating human emotions but on the divine will and word. Marriage is not invented by culture; it is established by creation. What God has established by creation, no culture will be able to destroy; it will destroy itself first!

Therefore a man shall leave his father and his mother and hold fast to his wife, and they shall become one flesh. (Gen. 2:24)

This is more than a human contract; it is a divine covenant. It is exclusive, publicly declared, permanent, and consummated by sexual intercourse. (And the order of events is by God's design.)

The lordship of Jesus is to be on display not only in the public arena but in the privacy of our homes where, for better or worse, we are ourselves. Our marriages at best should be an advertisement for the Christian faith. If Christianity is going to make an impact on society, it must be seen to revolutionize our family life.

We are all in need of help in these matters. We need our local church family to teach us and train us and to remind us of God's enabling grace. A good marriage is in one respect like a golf swing in that it is not easy but it is straightforward. Only in Jesus do we find freedom from the distortions created by sin, including in our marriages. My wife and I are greatly encouraged by this book. It is a privilege to be able to commend it to you in this way.

Alistair Begg, Parkside Church, Chagrin Falls, Ohio

Introduction

THIS IS A BOOK FOR COUPLES, but not just couples. The institution of marriage is an integral part of the life of the Christian church. Time spent thinking about marriage will help some of us be more thoughtful about married life and all of us be more prayerful. For that reason, we appeal directly to married people throughout, but we also have in mind those who are only thinking about marriage or who want to support married people. There are no R-rated scenes. There are only helps for the married, prompts for those who want to pray, and encouragements for those who wish to defend and promote the institution of marriage, this gift from God that every church member ought to treasure, whether married or not.

This book has three main features that distinguish it from many other books on marriage. The most obvious is its brevity—busy people will find in only a few pages both a biblical defense of marriage and a practical guide to married life.

A second feature of this book is its frank assessment of who we are and of what we are capable. Many modern books on the Christian life acknowledge that Christians are sinners. In these pages we remind readers that Christians are also saints (to use a common New Testament term). Connected to Christ our Savior, we are called and enabled by his grace to love others, including our spouse.

The third unique aspect of this book is the path that it charts, for here we follow an old insight recovered from a book written four hundred years ago. The book, by a pastor named William Gouge, is quaintly entitled *Domestical Duties*. Not everything in it is helpful, but some things are, and in these few pages we pass on the best of what we've learned and are trying to put into practice.

In considering this book we also owe a debt of gratitude to our parents; to Craig and Carol Troxel, who gave us our premarital counseling; to the couples who have sat through our counseling; to the friends who read drafts of the book (notably Greg and Ginger O'Brien, Pat Daly, Justen and Catherine Ellis, Paul and Joy Woo, and Carlton and Linley Wynne); and to the two groups who heard versions of these chapters delivered in adult education sessions, first at Grace Presbyterian Church in Virginia and then later at Calvary Presbyterian Church in Pennsylvania. Your contributions have blessed readers with a better book.

1

The Bible and Marriage

Benjamin Franklin is credited with the wry comment that people should have their eyes wide open before marriage and half shut afterward. There is truth in both halves of the saying, but we want to talk about the "eyes wide open" part. What should we be looking for if we, or others close to us, are thinking about marriage?

One Man and One Woman

It turns out that the first thing that we should look for in a marriage is someone of the opposite sex. There is such a thing as male and female, and it is not merely a personal or social construct. We can see it in the way in which we are made, and the Bible points it out even before it gets to the topic of relationships: Genesis 1 introduces us to "male and female"; people who are in some ways the same (being made in the image of God) and in some ways different (intended to complement one another).

The idea of sex or gender is important, but not in isolation. One message of the opening chapter of the Bible is that the pinnacle of creation is not one but two, and they go together. "God created man . . . male and female" (Gen. 1:27).

So men and women are meant to be paired. That is an important start. But when God chose to have *The Talk* with Adam, he introduced important additional information, for God talked about a man leaving his father and mother and cleaving to his wife. The words that God chose are significant, for they twice emphasize not only the proper sex for marriage, but the right number. First he says that a parental pair is to consist of a father and a mother. Then he says that marriage is supposed to be between a husband and a wife (Gen. 2:24).

Every Christian knows that even a hint of God's revealed will should be considered with utmost seriousness. And in Genesis 2 God gave much more than a hint: it is God's will for a man to have one wife, and for a woman to have one husband, and for neither to have more than one at the same time. Obviously the idea of one plus one was a command for Adam and Eve. After all, at least at first, they were the only human beings around. But clearly this was meant as a command for all future generations, even if it was hardly kept with any faithfulness. Sometimes people have taken more than one spouse at a time. All too often they have exchanged one spouse for another.

In some cases, remarriage is a gift from God for a wounded man or woman, and often for the children too. We can thank God for this gracious provision. But marriage is normally to be a lifelong commitment, and Jesus himself emphasized the God-given creational pattern for marriage, established in Genesis 2, with a warning that what God has put together, we must not separate (Mark 10:9).

Not Holy, but Special

So marriage is for a man and a woman. Any single man can marry a single woman. One does not need to be a Christian to make promises approximating what Malachi calls a marriage "covenant" (Mal. 2:13–16). Marriage is a civil ordinance, not a Christian sacrament. It is special, but it is not sacred. "Let marriage be held in honor among all," the book of Hebrews tells us (Heb. 13:4).[1] The apostle Paul warns against those who forbid people to marry (1 Tim. 4:3). Quite the opposite attitude should be on display in the Christian community: we ought to encourage people—Christians or not—to choose the most visible, most committed form of marriage that a culture has. Christians need to be advocates for marriage maximalism, not marriage minimalism, as is the unhappy trend in some modern societies.

We live in a culture where sex, living together, and even marriage are often about getting rather than giving. This is most obviously true out of marriage, as wiser cultural pundits have noted. Cohabiting couples eventually realize that they are always auditioning or interviewing as potential marriage partners, especially in the bedroom. Such relationships rest on unwritten contracts. Whether people realize it or not, there is a sense in which they are commercialized, continuing only as long as each side gets what it wants.

Some cultures err in redefining who can be married or in undermining the usefulness and beauty of marriage. In rejecting these redefinitions or reevaluations, Christians cannot simply appeal to tradition. We must not simply exchange the misguided conventions of our day for the conventions of another age or place, including those of other cultures or older societies. After all, there have been and still are societies where convention encourages people to be given in marriage even though one or both parties lacks the maturity and wisdom to make the decision or to consent to an arrangement. In the 1640s the English parliament rejected the idea, promoted by Puritan ministers, that people should marry only if they are able to exercise proper judgment and give their own consent. Today some religions and cultures would also object to these provisos. And thinking of tradition, it is perhaps here that we should add that Christians are also free to marry without respect to race, ethnic origins, and nationality, no matter what our cultural norms might be. Once marriage for the people of God was restricted to Israelites only. To be a follower of God one had to become a Jew and marry a Jew. Now we are as free as anyone to marry anyone in the Lord.

If we are to find a reliable model for marriage, we will need to do better than appeal to cultural norms, past or present. Marriage is for both Christians and non-Christians, but nonetheless, in developing a definition of marriage, Christians must go back to Scripture as their guide. A proper understanding of this gift from God, already emerging in our brief study, is that marriage is a lifelong, exclusive, and publicly recognized bond between a man and a woman. That this bond is an intimate one is implied by its exclusivity, but we will discuss intimate relations more thoroughly in a later chapter.

We'd like to add that marriage always ought to be consensual too, but here Scripture constrains us. There are hints in both the Old and New Testaments that a freedom of choice in marriage is a good thing. If we turn to the Old Testament, it is hard to escape the sense that part of the beauty of the story of Isaac and Rebekah is that she was given a choice to marry this son of Abraham and bravely decided to do so (Gen. 24:57–58). As well, if we look at the possible options facing engaged couples in 1 Corinthians 7:36–38 it is not clear that the apostle Paul is discussing a parentally arranged marriage; it seems as if he is teaching potential partners how to make informed judgments about a betrothal or engagement. But we would be saying too much if we said that an arranged marriage is by definition not a true marriage. That said, we should probably mention in this context that age matters in all marriages. Marital union should take place only after puberty, for it is adults and not children who are to marry. And while we are on the topic of age, we should stress that proposed marriages with wide age discrepancies must be considered very carefully lest the purpose of marital companionship be marginalized or even jeopardized.

Two Believers

There is another reason why Christians are in favor of consent in marriage. And that is because Christians who want to marry have the responsibility of marrying other Christians. We get hints early in the Old Testament that further guidance was needed for God's people who were seeking a spouse. Some additional discernment was required in a relationship beyond identifying a coordinate gender.

The clues add up quickly. In Genesis we are told that those identified as God's people *did not wish* to marry the unbelieving people who were conveniently living around them. In Exodus we are informed that they *should not* marry from the nations around them. It is too simplistic to say that the issue was merely racial. With increasing clarity, we are told that a follower of the Lord must not marry a follower of "foreign gods" because it will draw him or her away from a true loyalty to the one who made us, preserves us, even saves us (Deut. 6:10–7:5).

Now sometimes people face difficult circumstances. Esther did not choose her husband. Given the choice to marry someone who did not believe in the true God or face likely death, she married (Est. 1–2). Often people become Christians while they are married. If possible, they should remain married (1 Cor. 7). And yet, tragically, many who profess faithfulness to the Lord are willing to marry unbelievers under very different circumstances. They imagine that they are so strong that the unbeliever will be won over by their faith. "He will come my way." Or, "I won't drift her way." The whole history of the nation of Israel says that the opposite is true. We ignore these lessons to our peril.

A Christian considering marriage must be clear about this basic requirement. Christians must assure themselves that they are marrying a Christian, and they must have solid grounds for such a conclusion. Of course, we cannot guarantee that people will continue to walk with the Lord. But we can ask good questions about their walk before we decide to commit: Does our prospective marriage partner clearly confess Christ? Does he or she make use of the gifts God has given for us to grow, like Bible reading, good preaching, the sacraments, and Christian fellowship? Does he or she pray? Do we find ourselves growing closer to the Lord as a result of this friendship?

The question of whether to marry a believer or an unbeliever is not merely a matter of wisdom. This is a matter of obedience, for it is the plain teaching of the Bible. After Paul discusses marriage and remarriage in 1 Corinthians 7, he assures his readers that they are free to marry anyone, as long as he or she belongs to the Lord (1 Cor. 7:39). In other words, all other arrangements, no matter what the motive, are forbidden.

We can say more than that. Christians should find a life partner who is a member of a church that clearly loves and preaches the gospel—in fact, preaches the whole counsel of God, since all of that will be needed for a useful Christian life and a strong Christian marriage. Sometimes God so orders the events of our lives that Christians find themselves alone in prayer, alone in reading the Bible, alone in the pew. Sometimes we cannot help but have only one parent praying at a child's bedside, one parent bringing a child to church, one parent praying for faith and repentance, one parent prioritizing what is eternal over what is temporal—and all the while the other parent is silently not supporting, or even vocally opposing, these things. In God's providence this does happen. But for a Christian to plan this—to enter a situation where this is the case while hoping that one day it might not be the case? This is foolish, and God loves us so much that he forbids us from doing this (see 2 Cor. 6:14).

We need to remind ourselves, and sometimes we need to remind others, that if the concept of "evangelistic dating" has plausibility, or even fascination, for us or for our friends, this is in itself a sign of weakness, not of strength. It shows that our hearts are already privileging a relationship in this world over the one relationship that can live on into the next world. Members of cults flirt to convert. Christians must not use romance for outreach. We have already lost if we think that we can honor God by disobeying him. Let us put Jesus Christ first in our lives, and then we will find guidance in our engagements and a model for our marriages.

What Is Marriage For?

Knowing who and how many people should be in a marriage, even to offer guidelines for Christian marriage partners, doesn't yet say what marriage is for. Once again, the beginning of an answer is already found in the first book of the Bible.

Marriage is for mutual support, companionship, reproduction of the human race, and the promotion of sexual purity. For Christians, we can also add that marriage is for church growth, for offering a context for children to be nurtured in the Christian faith, and for reflecting the relationship between Christ and the church (Eph. 5). And it is worth noting that all of this is more about giving than getting, an important idea that we'll return to in later chapters.

Going back to Genesis, God paraded every kind of creature in front of Adam not only so that he could help rule the world in naming the animals, but also so that it would be crystal clear that no random mammal could help and support him. For that, he needed a wife. He and his wife needed one another for company. For many centuries, even millennia, the fact that man and woman were to be friends, companions, was not emphasized in marriage narratives. But while Adam and Eve were to work together in this world, at a more basic level, they were called to *be* together.

Together, they were also to be fruitful and to multiply the human race. We see this in God's command in Genesis 1, which helps us to understand the importance of parenting. Sometimes couples cannot give birth to children. But there needs to be an extraordinary reason for them to refuse to have children.

God also provides marriage as the only context for sexual activity and purity. About this, Scripture could not be clearer. Marriage was created at a time when there was no immorality, but it continues in a time where every kind of sexual problem abounds. In this world some can manage lifelong purity apart from marriage. Many will find this difficult, and they should make it their ambition to marry (1 Cor. 7:2, 9). That also means that people contemplating marriage—an exclusive relationship intended to promote purity and a context in which they will be trying to make babies together—should marry someone *they* find attractive, including physical attraction. Someone they love in every way.

So sex and number matter in marriage. Race and nationality should not. Friendship counts because we want companionship. Looks matter only to the looker. Age matters too. But most of all, a real and living faith must matter to every Christian who wishes by God's grace to be faithful. These are the biblical foundations of a Christian marriage.

2

History and Marriage

RECOMMENDED READING

GENESIS 3

There is sometimes an urgent reason why people pick up a book on marriage. You may already have skimmed the contents page and jumped into a chapter or two that addresses an immediate need. Perhaps, without telling your husband or wife, you headed straight to the appendix, where we offer everything we know about accelerating the work of the Holy Spirit in the life of a spouse. We get that. But we have a reason for these opening chapters. They give us the big picture so that we can place the topic of marriage in proper perspective.

Perspective

Getting a big-picture perspective on marriage seems like an obvious to-do. But what is the big picture? Is it psychological? Marriage books will tell you that your perspective on marriage depends on whether you're a glass-half-full person or a glass-half-empty person. Is it biological? Does your fundamental orientation for marriage depend on whether you are a man or a woman? There is enormous importance to these factors, among others. Nonetheless, the most important (and perhaps the most overlooked) perspective on marriage is historical, specifically, the history of God's gracious redemption of his people, and our place in it.

Augustine of Hippo famously wrote that the history of humanity is divided into four stages, and it seems to us that there are practical reasons why we need to consider the nature of marriage in its fourfold state. In fact, knowing we are part of this matrix gives us the perspective that we'll need for the coming chapters.

So let's look at marriage in redemptive history. First the garden-variety marriage. Then the fallen marriage. This will be followed by marriage on the way. And, finally, we'll consider the consummate marriage.

The Garden-Variety Marriage

In its initial state, marriage was as perfect as it could be. Adam and Eve were able to sin but also able not to sin, and for a time they made the right choice. It was the "1 Corinthians 13 definition" of love lived out to perfection. It sounds not only ideal, but Edenic.

Of course the kind of love that Paul describes in 1 Corinthians 13 includes the kind of love that is possible in a good friendship; it is not for married people only. Nonetheless, it captures what the garden-variety marriage in a perfect world would look like. The kind of love Paul pictures is patient and kind. Negatively, this love is not jealous; it does not boast; it is not proud, arrogant, rude, self-seeking, or irritable. This love is not resentful; it sees no wrongs and delights in the good. Positively, married love in the garden can be captured by Paul's string of superlatives: it "bears all things, believes all things, hopes all things, endures all things" (13:7). This is the kind of love that would offer as much joy for the one loved as for the one loving.

And it could have kept on going. They were able to sin. But also able not to sin. It is hard for people, even people in the best of marriages, to imagine anything so perfect. It was probably even more impossible for the first couple to imagine anything less perfect.

The Fallen Marriage

People tend not to be good at thinking through negative consequences; this is a human limitation. Adam and Eve didn't think things through, and they suddenly found out what it was like *not* to be able not to sin. In this second stage in world history these lost sinners did not have a gospel in which to hope.

In that dark hour of hiding from God and each other, they had no knowledge of any plan of salvation, only knowledge of condemnation. They used to want to please God and please each other. But immediately after the first taste of sin, the first married pair stopped encouraging each other in their fellowship with God. Within no time at all, they had their first fight: we overhear them evading responsibility, blaming the other for their sin. At the first sign of danger, they were no longer protecting but were instead betraying each other.

Their marriage would forever be colored by the knowledge that left to their own, they not only turned their backs on the Lord but also turned their backs on each other. In other words, in a fallen world there is fallen marriage, and couples will hurt, disappoint, and provoke one another.

In this fallen world, we should expect sin in a marriage. In some marriages, it seems like it is all that is seen. As Augustine put it, they are *not* able not to sin. There are so many homes where grace is unknown. These are marriages where words are calculated to raise the temperatures of those around them; where hearts are often shelters for unloving thoughts, providing a haven for hundreds of bitter memories. There are so many marriages paired with irritable, arguing, bitter partners; men and women in relationships where anger seethes beneath the surface and where violence erupts at any time. These are people who do not know the one who is slow to anger and abounding in love.

This is a picture of marriage where people are only able to sin. But you already know that we must be bold enough to qualify Augustine's description just a little. For we all know that unbelieving people are not as bad as they can be. After all, Adam and Eve argued with one another, but they did not go on to kill one another. And it was not that they could do no good; they did speak some truth when they answered God's questions. Countless people who do not know the gospel are kept by God from complete marital meltdowns and are even granted real marital happiness. There is something theologians call "common grace"—where God restrains us from our sin—and we see this at work in marriages all around us.

But the heart of Augustine's observation still stands. Even in those cases, the currency of kindness is foreign; it is borrowed but not really owned. And the real point is that every aspect of our marriages will be marred by sin, and people will be helpless to truly forgive, helpless even to change themselves without God's help.

Apart from the grace of God, a husband wants his wife to excuse his sin while he in turn will not want to excuse hers. A wife may focus her efforts on changing her husband rather than changing herself. The deep point at stake is that fallen people do not submit to God's law nor can they do so (Rom. 8:7). Every shining act of kindness for her will have buried beneath it a plan for him. Every act of love for another will paper over a love for self.

Marriage on the Way

Marriage was very different after the fall than it was before the fall. It was to change once again at the giving of the gospel, at least for those who have received Christ.

Praise God, he did not leave his creation alone in its broken, hopeless state. He promised Adam and Eve that he would send a descendant of theirs to save the world, and then he did so in sending his Son, Jesus Christ, who became a son of Adam in the womb of the virgin Mary (Gen. 3:15; Matt. 1:18–25; Luke 3:23–38). Then, in a blessing for all his people, he also sent his Holy Spirit, who applies the benefits Christ earned for his people through his life, death, and resurrection. Those who trust this Son and who rely on this Spirit enter yet another state. They become able not to sin.

Unlike the first stage in our history, in this third stage we are unable to completely stop sinning. Or to put it another way, our ability not to sin is limited and imperfect. But, again, the center of Augustine's summary holds for those who have Christ as Savior. By God's grace we can actually please our Father in heaven. In Christ, our motives and actions are increasingly purified. Now our acts of love for others are less and less fueled by a love for ourselves.

We hope you can already see how this cruise through history should shape the way in which we think about marriage. Let us sum up our three stages thus far. First, we are not in paradise.

Second, ever since the fall, married people have had problems. Emily recalls one time in the early months of marriage when Chad was doing something particularly annoying. Emily was caught off guard and had to remind herself, "Oh, yes, he's a sinner." And, third, for those who know the Father's forgiving grace in Christ and the transforming power of the Holy Spirit, there is actually hope. We don't need to panic or despair when we discover we have marriage trouble. God redeems married people too.

Chad does most of the despairing on behalf of the two of us. It's one of his jobs, because we each play to our strengths. Emily is the prayer partner; Chad is the despair partner (which is hardly fair, he says, because at the same time he causes much of the trouble). But despair is unhelpful, even sinful. The truth is that we are not helpless victims destined to fruitless suffering nor hopeless aggressors, unable to stop saying and doing things that hurt our spouse.

Our marriages in this third stage are marriages on the way. They are pilgrim marriages. When Christians are hopeless, we are forgetting that we are no longer in the garden after our first parents' sin and before the giving of the gospel. We are not stuck in the moments or hours before God promised to crush the serpent. No, we are living on the other side of God's promise to send a seed of Adam to be our Savior; we are living on the other side of the cross, of the empty tomb, of disciples looking with wonder up into heaven and looking to Christ in faith. We live in the age of the Spirit, whose enabling power gives grace to sinners who long to love others as Christian saints should.

Perhaps you know of someone whose marriage isn't that great. Maybe you yourself are all too aware that your spouse is a sinner, and you feel stuck. You may feel let down or even betrayed. Your marriage is not all you expected it would be.

Well, redemptive history has something to teach us: for those who know Christ, marriages really can get better—both the bad marriages and even the good ones. Maybe yours is so bad that you are tempted to think, "If only I weren't married, life would be great!" The history of redemption has something to say here too. On the one hand, our relational problems are a universal consequence of the fall, married or not. On the other hand, God promises to use the troubles of Christians to make us more like Christ every time that we turn to him. Long-term relationships give us a laboratory where we get to see how forgiveness, perseverance, and change work. This makes marriage a great place to glorify God.

Perhaps you yourself are the ball and chain to marital progress. If so, remember that God is in the business of changing people. Reread the apostle Paul's story. God promises to take every sinner who trusts in him and conform him to the image of Christ. We don't all make the same level of progress, but no believer is left behind. Jesus didn't come for those who are healthy. He came for the sick. And by his gospel power, he has taken unhealthy marriages and so radically transformed them in his good time that they have come to image the relationship between Christ and his bride, the church (Eph. 5).

So in this stage of redemptive history Christians can—Christians must—encourage one another with the promise of God's forgiveness and learn to forgive as we've been forgiven. At this time, too, we can learn what it means to be changed and to be God's instruments of gracious change in the life of our loved one.

Nonetheless, there is one more very important lesson that we are to learn.

The Consummate Marriage

As we consider marriage in its fourfold state, there is a lesson we need to learn in our current stage in redemptive history, but we learn it by looking ahead to the fourth and final stage of history—that period when we will no longer be able to sin, when will see rightly, as we were meant to see.

It is a lesson that Adam and Eve would have known instinctively at the moment of their creation.

It is a lesson that Adam and Eve unlearned at the moment they sinned.

It is a lesson that we gradually relearn as redeemed people, newly reoriented back to God.

It is a lesson that unmarried as well as married people need to learn. Simply put, while marriage is important, it's not everything. We know that, because there will be a final state in redemptive history where marriage will be transformed once more.

You may remember when Jesus rebuked the teachers of his day for not realizing that in heaven, men and women will be like the angels, neither married nor given in marriage (Matt. 22:30). Along the way, Jesus was pointing out what people were supposed to have figured out a long time before: human marriage is made in heaven, but not retained in heaven.

Christians often have very different reactions to this promise on the part of Jesus. But Jesus was saying something that every Christian must own for him- or herself. The marriage of eternity is better than the marriage of time. In heaven, the all-fulfilling relationship will not be between man and woman, but between God in Christ and the church as his bride. It was not good for Adam to be without Eve in the garden, but it will be fine for him to be without her in the new heavens and the new earth. Marriage is eternal in its significance, not because it lasts for eternity, but because it can be used to equip us for eternity.

We need to understand these historical facts about marriage for at least two reasons.

First, there are those for whom marriage carries overtones of unhappiness. Some Christians are unmarried. They must not think they will be missing something in heaven, just as some of them feel like they are missing something on earth. Some Christians are remarried, and Jesus is telling them they won't need to choose a favorite spouse. And some Christians need to remember Jesus's words because too little came of their marriage. The unhappily married will not be stuck with the loser they bore with in this life.

Along those lines, we both recall a very godly, cheerful, helpful woman who was married to one of the grouchiest people we had ever met. Thankfully, her life encouraged Emily to say to herself, "If she isn't complaining about her husband, I certainly shouldn't complain about mine!" But the more important lesson this woman taught us was that she could bear with all of this because she was heavenly minded. Her marriage was placed in a larger redemptive-historical context; she was more married to Jesus than she was to the cantankerous man who lived at her address. She knew that every kind of marriage is meant to prepare us for the last marriage.

Second, some of us need to remember this because we have come to idolize our marriage. We have been given a wonderful marriage, and we are tempted to give it a place it does not deserve.

We have built hopes on a woman or looked for happiness in a man that ultimately can only be fulfilled by God himself.

Of course a beautiful marriage is a God-given gift. A Christian marriage even pictures the relationship between Christ and the church. But that is the point: a good marriage is only intended to point us to a better one. Part of Christian faithfulness is seeing that only a relationship with Christ is ultimate. Do you believe that? We believe it—but we ask the Lord to help us in our unbelief.

Sometimes Christians act like only the "spiritually elite" need to believe that marriage does not continue in heaven. We want to suggest that it is one of the most basic things that a child of God must believe.

Adam put Eve before God, thinking it would make them happier. It didn't. So God's history of redemption, building to its final climax, tells us that marriage isn't the perfect gift that will make us happy (on the one hand), or a load of problems to be fixed or endured (on the other). The word of God preaches against both the idol of our hearts and the cynic of our souls.

But when God said that it was not good for Adam to be alone, he never meant for him to think that he could do with Eve alone— not in any ultimate sense. Already in the garden, walking with the Lord in the cool of the day should have meant more to Adam and Eve than cleaving to each other in the middle of the night.

Advertisements from the wedding industry are all about the perfect day. Every effort is to be made to prepare a bride for marriage. Every expense that can be afforded is to be spent. What we need to see is that God from the beginning has gone through every effort to prepare for the wedding supper of the Lamb. In fact no expense was spared. The bride was washed clean by nothing less than the blood of God's own Son, and the Father and the Son together send the Holy Spirit to make the bride presentable for the feast.

When all ordinary marriages come to an end, this momentous marriage will last for eternity. Whether single or married on earth, all believers will be included in this final consummation. No marriage courses or books will be needed. All will be forever perfect in the bond between the one church and the one God.

The fact that our marriages here will end doesn't make marriage in this life meaningless or work on our marriage fruitless. It just puts it into a larger purpose and a final perspective. We were designed above all for relationship with the Lord. The greatest moment in history will be when the resurrected body of the bride will meet her resurrected Savior face-to-face. This is why even the best moments in a marriage always have a shadow; a touch of imperfection; a haunting reminder that it will not last. There is only one marriage that is perfect and that knows no end. That is the truth and the promise that will lie behind everything that follows in the next few chapters. It puts Christian marriage into full perspective.

3

Grace in Marriage

RECOMMENDED READING

EPHESIANS 5:15–21

One of the Bible's best-known models for gracious relationships was penned by an unmarried man: the apostle Paul. He could offer grace for marriage because teaching about marriage does not need to be based on experience. In fact, if someone understands the gospel well, he or she will have insight into all kinds of relationships. The apostle's inspired insights are found in Ephesians 5, a key biblical passage on marriage.

Understanding Ephesians 5

Surprisingly, the whole of Paul's teaching in Ephesians 5 is prefaced by a verse about submission. What does *submission* mean to you? Many Christian people hear the word and it reminds them of a happy, reasonably well-ordered home. They think of a place where authority was exercised in a benevolent way, and for their good. Other people (again, including many Christians) hear the word, and they bristle or cringe. Under the banner of submission they have seen bullies belittle and abuse women and children.

We all know that this has gone on for centuries, and in many cultures it is the aggressor and not the victim who is protected by religious and civil laws.

Negative experiences may impact initial reactions to the idea of submission. But we cannot adopt or reject the act of submitting based on past experiences. And that is because of Ephesians 5:21. There, as the apostle Paul describes the fruit of a life filled with the Holy Spirit, he mentions one last item: after listing things like worshiping and thanking, he commends "submitting to one another out of reverence for Christ." So submission is part of the standard package of the Christian life just as much as the practice of worship or a posture of thankfulness. This is clear in standard translations of verse 21; submission is not an optional extra that we custom-order for people who are unusually spiritual or who have untroubled family backgrounds.

And yet while Ephesians 5:21 is not difficult to translate, it is challenging to locate. On the one hand, it is connected to the verses before it. So some translations place verse 21 at the end of a paragraph that goes before it (vv. 15–21). On the other hand, Paul did not give verse 22 a stand-alone verb of its own, and thus it is forced to borrow one from verse 21. That is why other translations place verse 21 at the beginning of the paragraph that follows it (vv. 21–24). Of course there are also translations that split the difference, leaving verse 21 stranded and alone, married to neither paragraph.

Placement of Ephesians 5:21 has led to a stalemate. But almost everyone sees the importance of this passage as a pivotal point in Paul's instruction. Looking back from the verse, we see that the Holy Spirit requires submission on the part of all Christian people. Looking forward, we see how submission is important as we study the role of wives and also the roles of husbands, parents, children, masters, and servants.

Submission Is for Everyone

In our introduction we mentioned William Gouge's book *Domestical Duties*. Gouge wisely dedicated many of his pages to the importance of Ephesians 5:21 and the call to mutual submission "out of reverence for Christ." Significantly Gouge did not do this because he felt awkward about verse 22 and its specific mention of the submission of wives. He did so because he wanted to take seriously the message of verse 21 on its own terms. He wanted to understand what mutual submission might look like.

What Gouge was trying to do in his generation is important for us to do in ours. Before we get to particular responsibilities in marriage, we need to see what is common to all of us.

In the first place, we need to think aloud about the kind of submission that the Holy Spirit has in mind for the Christian church. Negatively, we can note that the submission talked about here is rooted in creationism, not chauvinism.[2] It is something we get from our Maker. Christians are not blindly to reflect societal conventions. We should not believe in the idea of submission because everybody else likes it, and we should not reject the idea because everybody else doesn't. On the contrary, we need to believe that if God requires something, then it is necessary for our flourishing, maybe even for our survival. He always calls us to what will lead us to praise him and toward what is in itself good, true, and, properly understood, beautiful.

Positively, and in the second place, we need to own that whatever submission is, we are all in this together. Not only do we all need to submit to God; we need to submit to each other. Submission is for everyone. That is the point of verse 21, which helps to set the stage for this discussion of marriage. In fact it sets the stage for each of the three scenarios that Paul addresses in this letter: marital relations, parental relations, and labor relations. In some way, each of these relationships ought to involve a profound respect that leads to a willingness to serve others. On one level, submitting is respecting that leads to serving.

Practically, if Christians are going to pull off submission in a world that hates the word, it will mean that our marriages must be characterized by mutual respect, care, and service—a kind of quiet competition to put the other person first. A "you first," "please let me get that for you" attitude. It is this third point that leads us to consider the importance of thoughtfulness in a marriage where sinners are seeking to be sanctified in their interactions with their spouse.

The Thoughtful Marriage: Knowing Each Other

If we are going to submit to one another, we need to know each other. That means a commitment to studying one another. Knowing how she thinks or what he loves, identifying her likes or his needs. In submitting to one another, we are loving each other by studying each other. The most responsive servants are the most attentive ones. You may have seen this with top-notch servers in restaurants or the ideal attendant on a flight.

Chad is committed to this kind of study of Emily, even if it remains very much in progress. He often remembers a painful morning, about eleven years into our marriage, when he offered Emily some orange juice with her breakfast, and, as usual, asked her if she would like any ice in her glass. He recalls the details of what followed like it was yesterday: "We were both standing at the kitchen counter, and she looked at me sweetly and asked how long we had been married. That was the first sign that something was going sideways. The second indicator of trouble came when she asked me, very sweetly, if I had asked her this before. And of course I had, almost every morning for the last decade. The clincher came when she asked me, with a teeny bit less sweetness, if she had *ever*, to my knowledge, said yes."

Behind the Early Morning Orange Juice Incident, or EMOJI, to coin a term, was some ignorance on Chad's part. But also behind the EMOJI was a lack of attentiveness to Ephesians 5:21 (but we will resist the strange impulse to add a sad face here).

Whatever was going on in his heart, he needed to take more seriously Ephesians 5. He didn't say that then. When EMOJIs happen in a marriage—and this was not the first one—we first want to blame our short memories, our busyness, or someone's fickleness (Chad does think that Emily asked for ice during pregnancy. She asked for everything at least once).

But the same pattern can recur or reemerge with more serious matters. So if we are to be faithful to the Holy Spirit speaking to us in his word, we need to see submission as a spiritual gift that the Lord values. If we did, spouses would be more willing and better able to submit our time, memory, and energies to serving each other, and we'd have fewer EMOJIs (which we hope you'd agree would be a good thing).

Studying one another in marriage, getting to know each other, involves every aspect of life. It is a lifelong process. This is why we tell our life stories. This is one more reason why Christian couples should ask how they can pray for each other in the morning. This is why we do well to ask at the end of the day, "How was your day?" and to actually listen to the report. It is not simply to discover our to-do list or action points. It is part of a process of knowing each other.

The Bible recognizes this, indeed teaches us this, in the very vocabulary that it uses to describe one part of our marital relations. Newer translations of the Bible refer to husbands and wives "having sex." Older translations refer to the same set of actions as husbands and wives "knowing" each other, which better reflects the Hebrew of the Old Testament. There is real significance to that phrase, especially in that intimate context. But whether speaking about the intimate or the mundane, knowing a spouse in order to serve a spouse is one of the most enjoyable, rewarding, and challenging gifts that we can give in a marriage.

The Gracious Marriage: Knowing Scripture

Honoring Ephesians 5:21 entails knowing a spouse. Even more important—it involves knowing Scripture. Or to put it another way, we must study not only our spouse's likes and needs, but we must also study their duties before the Lord. Oddly enough, a successful study of someone else's duties, for the right reasons, should facilitate a gracious marriage.

It is at just this point that William Gouge's insights have been so helpful for marriage (and family). He offers an angle, or a principle, that we find very helpful.

Have you ever wondered why the apostle Paul here, and Scripture everywhere, tells all of us about everyone else's duties, as well as our own? Why in Ephesians 5 does a wife get to hear how a husband should behave? For that matter, why in Ephesians 6 are children permitted to know that their father is not supposed to provoke them in his approach to parenting? Why does a servant get to hear God threaten masters about threatening their servants?

One obvious answer is that the same Bible was intended for everyone. We are used to a proliferation of Bibles for students, Bibles for singles, and Bibles for mothers with toddlers between the ages of two and four. We are used to a flavor of study Bible for every kind of person. The Bible itself is not written that way. It is a one-text-speaks-to-all kind of book, so we get to overhear instruction for everyone.

Another seemingly obvious answer might be that we know about everyone else's duty so that we can remind them where they fall short, and then tell them to do a better job. We've seen this often in marriage. We've done this in marriage. Apart from the grace of God, this is our default position as Bible readers. A husband reads Ephesians 5:22 so that he can better instruct his wife how to submit to him. A wife reads verse 25 for return ammunition: he is supposed to love her! Parents hammer Ephesians on the heads of their children, reminding them to obey them in the Lord (often when we are most angry).

As you may have guessed, or learned from experience, this tends not to be especially effective. It is more helpful to see, with William Gouge, that Ephesians 5 is not an improvement guide for spouses (that is addressed in the appendix). On the contrary, we are told one another's duties for the purpose of making their work a joy to them—just as Scripture puts it, in another context, for ministers and church members (Heb. 13:17).

This is a very practical point. While working on this book Chad sinned against Emily. And then among other things, this came to mind: he considered how much easier it would be for her to respect him if he repented. And that began a turn in the right direction. We have been focusing on the importance of grace in our marriage. It has been a critical component of our premarital counseling too, even if couples cuddled on a couch rarely remember anything we say.

This is a practical point and a guiding principle for this book. Are husbands to love their wives (to pick one example of a duty)? Then wives are to make themselves as lovable as possible, for this is the principal way of helping a husband with his own duty to love her. Is a wife supposed to respect her husband? Then he needs to do his best to be worthy of respect in order to help her respect him.

We will flesh out in a later chapter the unique ways in which husbands and wives relate to the idea of submission and headship in the home, for mutual submission is not the whole story in a marriage. But for now, let us run with the example of husbands and mutual submission for a moment longer. If the husband is to help his wife, then he should affirm her equality as a person, show his esteem for her, provide for her as best he can, explain why he loves her from the heart, and be gentle, courteous, generous, and wise. All of this is mentioned by Gouge in his *Domestical Duties*. He argues at length that mutual submission, understood thoughtfully and graciously, calls a husband to try what he can to make the wife's task as much of a joy as possible. He should stand on his rights as infrequently as possible lest he wear them out. He should have a style of leadership that lives more than announces, and instead do all that is wise and right to emphasize the liberties she enjoys as a Christian woman.[3]

Reverence for Christ

The subtitle of this book, *Grace for Sinners to Love Like Saints*, speaks about grace for sinners because this kind of preoccupation on the part of both partners requires much grace—along with kindness and patience and joy—if we are to love like saints should. But what makes a marriage fundamentally gracious?

The answer to that question is the thread that stitches the whole of this passage on marriage together. What makes a marriage gracious is the price the Savior paid, the pattern the Savior offers, and the power the Savior provides.

Our Savior gave himself for us. He came to rescue a disobedient, unsubmissive people. People who too often look out for "number one." People who stand on their rights while talking about other people's duties. He came for selfish sinners like you and me. We really need to see this. Our Savior did not give himself to those who already gave themselves. He did not wait for us to do our duties. He is the Savior for those who fail in their duties while clamoring about their rights. Jesus Christ is the one who makes right before God every person who looks to Jesus, the one who submitted himself to the wrath of God and the punishment of death. Our marriages are gracious when we reverence Christ in them, when we see that the price the Savior paid covers our particular sins, including our sins in marriage.

In all of this, Jesus acts in our place and for our sake. But he also does these things as an example. In coming chapters we'll see how the letters of both Paul and Peter fill this out in very practical ways. Here it is enough to know that our marriages are gracious, and we reverence Christ in them when we seek to follow the perfect pattern that the Savior sets for us.

But what is the good of the best blueprint if we are unable to build with it? To answer this question we could go almost anywhere in the New Testament. But in this case we don't need to travel far. In his saving work Christ not only covers the cost of our restoration, but he unites us to himself—he makes us members of his body, Ephesians 5:30 says. And so with Christ we are dead to sin; with him we are raised with new power to a new life, including a new power for marriage. This too we must recognize in our marriages. Our marriages will be gracious, and we will reverence Christ in them, when we live in the power that the Savior provides. Let us praise him for this power and ask that we will show reverence for Christ in the way in which we love each other and submit to one another in all things, including marriage.

Women and Marriage

RECOMMENDED READING

EPHESIANS 5:22–24

Scripture calls each one of us to submit to one another, to display a deep respect that leads to thoughtful service. This is part of what it means to be "filled with the Spirit" and live in "reverence for Christ" (Eph 5:18, 21). These are common Christian duties, but they do not swallow up particular duties. Indeed Scripture goes on to explain how our mutual submission must play out in the distinct roles of husbands and wives. Thus this chapter and the next will consider these roles as we find them in Ephesians 5. Following that, we'll think about marital conflict as it is discussed in 1 Peter 3.

Heads, Not Tails

In his treatment of Christian marriage, the apostle Paul politely puts ladies first, as we can see in Ephesians 5:22, where he writes, "Wives, submit to your own husbands." The fact that this command is stated in verse 22, repeated in verse 24, and given a context in verse 23 only emphasizes its importance. So we had better understand what submission means!

Submission is respect that leads to serving. But in marriage, submission is also another aspect of love—to submit is to give yourself up for someone. To submit to someone is to make room for the other and his or her ideas. To submit is to listen and to follow. To submit is to put someone else first. To submit is to do what someone else asks, even when it is hard.

We need to submit to each other in every way, but Paul is saying that in a properly ordered home, the family does have a leader. God not only created husbands and wives; he also created the relationship between them. There is mutual submission in a marriage, *and* wives are to submit to and respect their husbands. According to verses 22–24, there is a sense in which a Christian wife is especially to shine in this grace. Something unique is going on. In fact, wives are to submit to their husbands, Paul tells us, "as the church submits to Christ" (5:24).

In other words, in a Christian marriage a wife has a respectful perspective toward her husband. She doesn't submit to her husband as if he has the wisdom and righteousness of Christ, but she has that *disposition* toward her husband. She does not submit to her husband to the same extent as she submits to Christ, but she has a submissive orientation toward her husband and all his wise and righteous intentions. So each wife is to know her own husband, to learn his preferences, his joys, his weaknesses; to be willing to listen and support him; to celebrate his strengths and be gracious about his failings. She is to be radically committed to respecting her husband and following his lead.

Wife, do you want your husband to love you and care for you? Then respect and love him, not reminding him of his duties but making his calling as easy as possible in a spirit of submission and esteem.

Do you want to make it easier for your husband to love you and respect you? Then do not shout, and complain, and excuse your sin. Be women of grace who admit your wrongs and model the gospel.

Do you want your husband to love you? Then honor him in a way that mirrors or reflects the honor that the church presents to Christ. Be willing to set aside your own ambitions and plans for him, even some of your pride.

To do this, a Christian wife does not need to agree that her husband's way is best in and of itself. If that were so, following would not be called "submission" but "agreement." The command is not *Agree with your husband*, but *Submit to him*. That does not mean returning to the era of the Flintstones or imagining the Jetsons. It is not the artificial "yes, dear" of yesteryear. It means a dignified, humble, loving gift of one's self to one's husband.

It is important to see that submission is more than a mere duty. It is not just one task that she does. No, submission refers to a role, even more than that, a perspective or orientation that characterizes how she does what she does.

The reason why we think this is true is that a wife is to submit to her husband "as to the Lord" (5:22). Now it is possible that "as to the Lord" simply means that wives are to submit only to the extent that a husband is asking what is right; that is, she is to submit to him when what he says or wants is in accordance with God's law. Certainly it is true that we must never obey a command that contradicts God's law, and the Bible teaches that elsewhere. But given the way in which Paul continues his instruction here, he must mean much more.

He must mean that the same attitude that goes into giving oneself to Jesus Christ should go into giving oneself to a husband.

He must mean that it is God's perfect plan for women to give themselves to their imperfect husbands in a way that echoes the creative, energetic, committed service that they give to their perfect Savior.[4]

Note, too, how this orientation in marriage is backed up by a model for marriage. Scripture turns here (and elsewhere) to the idea of headship (see also 1 Cor. 11:3, 11–12). The husband is the head of the wife in a way that Christ is the head of the church. And "as the church submits to Christ, so also wives should submit in everything to their husbands" (Eph. 5:24). It's not as though Jane submits to John as if he were Jesus. It is not that in acknowledging her husband as a head of a marriage that she becomes the tail, some vestige of the important person she once was. No, she is the body and thus an essential part of the relationship. At an earlier point in this epistle, the apostle Paul calls the church Christ's "body, the fullness of him who fills all in all" (Eph. 1:23). What a striking comment! Christ is the all-sufficient leader. How surprising to hear Christ's apostle speaking this way about his relationship to his bride. How helpful to us in our discussion of marriage!

In thinking about Ephesians 1:23, Matthew Henry's commentary on the Bible tries to explain Paul's point by analogy: What is a king without his kingdom? What is a head without a body? What is a mediator without all his people? John Calvin says that it is "as if a father should say, 'My house seems empty when I do not see my child in it.' A husband will say, 'I seem to be only half a man when my wife is not with me.'"[5]

When the apostle returns to the subject of Christ and his body later in the same letter, he doesn't mean anything less than this. There is a great deal of depth in this analogy and in the language of headship that the apostle uses in Ephesians 5. But what is more to the point, in submitting to her husband, a godly wife is also submitting to her Lord, who gave her that husband. In submitting to her husband, she is submitting to the one who delegated some authority in the home to the head of that home. As John Calvin helpfully comments, it is "not that the authority [of Jesus and a husband] is equal." The point is only that "wives cannot obey Christ without yielding obedience to their husbands."[6] In the marriage where a wife respects her husband, the Lord is honored. With all the happiness of a Saturday morning bargain hunter, Emily says that in giving herself to her husband, she gives honor to two for the price of one.

This idea clearly ties into Ephesians 5:23. There we are told that "the husband is the head of the wife." In fact the husband is the head of the wife "even as Christ is the head of the church, his body." In another chapter we'll consider what it means to think of the head and body metaphor that Paul uses here, for he fleshes it out in the following verses. Here we need to ask what kind of headship the Bible envisages and answer by looking at Christ himself.

At some level, every Christian instinctively understands that we see gentleness, compassion, wisdom, and love in Christ. We see a life of giving. He gave himself—his very life—for his body, the church. That's the model. Of course, Christ was saving his bride for life and eternity. Husbands do no such thing. Nonetheless we can see from this analogy, as John Stott puts it, that a Christian wife is designed to submit to a lover and not an ogre.[7]

This is the Christian plan for marriage. An apostle will speak elsewhere in the Bible to wives whose husbands are far from reasonable (1 Pet. 3:1–6). Scripture gives counsel and direction to women whose husbands are not Christians or who do not act in a Christian way. And Scripture has much to say to husbands directly (e.g., Eph. 5:25–33; 1 Pet. 3:7). But here we need to see the normal baseline of marriage and what it looks like to give oneself to another.

In Everything

Scripture call wives to "submit in everything to their husbands" (which is not the same as saying that all women are to submit to all men). A Christian wife will want to give and serve because Scripture says so, but also because she knows that a self-giving spirit will make her husband's task to love her that much easier. In fact it is only this love for God and husband that will give her joy in this calling.

Mind you, this is a two-way street. Although Paul calls wives to submission in every area, a wise husband should learn—quickly—how seldom he should *ask* for submission in every area, explicitly or even implicitly. This is God's grace at work in him: if submitting is her responsibility, he will seek to make this as easy for her as possible. When a husband sees that a wife is to submit in everything, his first thought should be about her challenge, and thus his restraint. Husbands should save direct appeals to headship and authority for only the most important matters in marriage. This might not work in your own context, but in our home the subject comes up only once a year or so, maybe once every few years.

That said, although we rarely discuss the order that God has designed for our marriage, a spouse wanting to honor holy Scripture may hear a husband appealing to authority by the manner in which he speaks, and husbands should try to be sensitive to this dynamic.

As we've said, ideally husbands and wives should be able to do the majority of their work without having to arm wrestle their way toward a conclusion. Nonetheless, either spouse should always feel free to call for conversation when something is unclear.

As a case in point, Emily recalls decorating our first home. She looked forward to buying fabric and picked out some lovely blue and white patterns. Her husband declared the colors depressing and made a case for green and red. But the punch line is not about submission. It's about the need for sensitivity in a marriage where a spouse is eager to serve and submit. Emily bought red and green curtains, and then to please a husband who liked things to match, she found red and green china, tables, chairs, pillows, and accessories.

Fatefully, about a year later we were invited out to dinner, and Chad commented on our friends' beautifully appointed home. Emily noted that the comment seemed genuine—Chad really did like our friends' sense of taste. So the questions started: "Chad, what color are the chairs?"

"Blue. Blue and white."

"How lovely—blue and white chairs. And the china?"

"Blue and white."

"And the couch?"

"Blue and white."

Emily did not make a big deal of it. By God's grace the artist in her had somehow made peace with the color pallet of our home. But we did learn how important it was for us to have a few more conversations about matters that matter to one or both of us. The truth is that the man of the house sometimes makes poor decisions, or expresses opinions with conviction, or offers judgments ill-formed or ill-founded, and in matters of much greater significance than decorating. So Emily looked for ways of deepening a conversation, offering different perspectives, and challenging Chad's ideas about finances, parenting, and family priorities, while still submitting to her husband in everything.

Challenges to Submission: "Who Does This Anymore?"

This chapter in this book does not address everything that Scripture says about marriage. We will not even be able to address everything said in Ephesians 5. We haven't yet turned to the subject of husbands. But you will know that many non-Christian friends, especially in Western society, complain about the Bible's teaching on submission in verses 22 and 24, and on headship in verse 23.

When the practice of submission is challenged, biblical Christians instinctively want to rush to the apostle's Paul's defense:

1. Biblical scholars flag the idea of mutual submission in verse 21 and note how this frames the discussion as a whole.
2. Historians point out Martin Luther's distinction between *persons* and *roles*: the Scriptures hold up an equality of persons among men and women, even if there are differences of roles among husbands and wives. (This is tragically misunderstood when people looking for equality try to be someone else, or act like someone of the other gender. Equal worth does not equate to identical roles.)

3. Preachers protest that headship applies to particular relations and not all relations. Properly understood, a wife is
   called to submit to her own husband, and not to men in
   general.
4. Bible readers of every kind can insist that the apostle Paul did
   not say that a wife's only attitude should be one of submission. Elsewhere he prioritizes married women loving their
   husbands (Titus 2:4). What a sad marriage it would be if it
   had mutual submission without mutual love.

But the primary purpose of Christian people is not to defend
the Bible, as if God needs our help. We are to trust the Bible, for
we need God's help. As Christians we must be convinced that if
God calls us to submission, it is for our greatest good and richest
blessing.

And why should we worry that this does not conform to our
current cultural norm? Nothing about the incarnation, resurrection, or the return of Jesus is pedestrian and normal, so why
should Christian marriage sit comfortably with current societal
expectations? Why not expect the Christian life to subvert and
challenge social trends, just as we expect Christian doctrine to do?

As it happens, there is nothing normal about Paul's perspective on marriage, because when he speaks to wives, and then to
husbands, he talks about their responsibilities. He says not a word
about rights. It is not that rights do not matter (see chapter 8 later
in this book). But the responsibility of Christian wives is not to
focus on what should be coming to them, but on what they can
give to their husband. We'll see something similar, but more of
it, in the following chapter when we address husbands.

Challenges with Submission: "It's Too Fuzzy!"

Christian believers will hear friends offer challenges to submission. Christians themselves will try not to do so. Nonetheless we may have our own challenges with submission as we try (in submission to Christ) to work out what this will look like in a Christian marriage.

Most often the struggles Christian wives have with submission swirl around a first challenge: it's just too fuzzy. It's sometimes hard to know what it should look like in a given situation. It's hard to address this difficulty because what submission looks like will in fact vary significantly from home to home. Husbands and wives have different gifts, different life experiences, different allocations of time and energy. Scripture does not require—does not even value—cookie-cutter Christians, each of us trying to look the same. God spare us from such mindless tedium! But in every Christian marriage the intention, the desire, the goals, will be the same: she will be oriented toward her husband's happiness and his every good endeavor. She will not live at cross purposes to him but will try to see things from his perspective.

If submission is an orientation in marriage, then a woman's decisions will take into consideration her husband's commitments and the fulfillment of their shared goals in the home. As William Gouge noted long ago, in a good marriage, and given time, most of this will happen instinctively. We do not wish for people to think that everything Gouge says is correct, but here, once again, he is helpful. Because a wife will know her husband, and want to please him, she'll gradually discover what to do.

We sometimes see this after a Sunday morning service. We invite a couple on the spot to come over for lunch (only because we are rarely organized enough to ask people over in advance). Sometimes they say that they'll talk about it and get back to us in a few minutes. Sometimes we see them looking at each other, trying to find out without using words, whether one or the other wants to risk an afternoon with the Van Dixhoorns. Although the wife is to submit to her husband, the way in which it actually works out is characterized by mutual interest and submission, because she wants to respect his wishes whatever the cost, and he in love does not want to put her through anything that would be difficult for her.

As marriages mature, it will be more and more obvious where to go for lunch, how much money should be given to the child asking for a donation at the door, whether to buy a new chair or to pick up something sitting on the side of the street. It will be more obvious when discipline should be left for Dad and when it is time to stay up late with your spouse or go to bed. In fact just as it is more natural over time to know what pleases the Lord, a Christian wife will learn over time what pleases her husband.

Challenges with Submission: "It's Too Easy!"

Unfortunately we cannot pretend that all of our problems stem from a lack of clarity or that all of our challenges with submission run in one direction. This is one of those places where we are so glad to be writing this book together, because the second problem with Christian submission is that it can sometimes be too easy.

When Emily wrote this down, Chad did not see it coming. But Emily says that when she is indecisive or wants to avoid responsibility, the idea of submission is very convenient. It is sometimes simpler for her to say, "I don't know; you decide!"

And for a Christian woman, there is the added benefit of feeling spiritual, for Ephesians 5:22 says, "Wives, submit to your own husbands."

Now don't misunderstand us. In godly submission there is protection and happiness for a wife and her children. She will be following the Lord's ways and looking for his blessing. She will not know the future, but she will at least know that she is following the pattern set for her in Scripture, the church-like submission that is commended to her in Ephesians 5. And yet the truth is, and Chad thinks he should have realized this earlier, that Emily sees that complacent deference to him can, perversely, be part of a pattern that is not healthy. It can have the unintended side effect of stunting her Christian growth. If she just does what he likes without engaging in any decision-making process herself, she doesn't learn to wrestle with right and wrong or to seek God's wisdom in the hard decisions.

Punting routine decisions to a husband can sometimes mean that a wife doesn't learn how to trust God with her choices and find peace in the Lord when the outcome is unpleasant or uncertain. Scripture speaks about the husband as the head in a marriage, and sometimes the idea of headship is all too convenient. Many decisions—indeed most decisions—are to be made under a husband's headship, but by a wife who is using her head.

Conversely, a husband will usually be helping himself, and sometimes his wife, when he makes it his pattern to ask his wife for her opinion or judgment on a matter. Wise men consult wise wives and, as much as possible, make decisions with their full concurrence, not to share the blame if it goes wrong, but to maximize the chance that it will go right.

Challenges with Submission: "It's Too Hard!"

If there is a third major challenge with submission, it is that it is too hard. For many wives, making decisions is not difficult or not difficult most of the time. There are no doubt situations in which a wife wants to make the call and feels inhibited by the idea of having to talk it out, or to risk the chance of a decision that she thinks is not best. She is sure that if there is a disagreement in the marriage, she will be in the right, a fact that sad experience has only reinforced. What is more, she may be equal or superior to him in intellect, in judgment, in education, or in experience. Never mind that the Bible stresses the equality of persons at creation and in redemption or that submission is for everyone. She finds headship a hard or inconvenient fact.

In the context of this difficulty, we should remember first that a wife's task is not tougher than the husband's—just wait until the next chapter!

Second, it must be acknowledged that some husbands are stupid, or at least compartmentally smart. It is unfortunate when husbands think themselves omnicompetent even after repeated failures. But if a husband is only unwise and not sinful in his choices, it may be the family's lot to be made more like Christ through suffering on account of a foolish husband or father. This is very hard. But the Lord uses hard things for good ends.

Third, we should admit that some husbands are deeply problematic; perhaps mentally unstable or intermittently drunk. Submitting in these situations cannot extend to putting oneself or one's family in harm's way. Physical and verbal abuse is Satan's plan for a marriage, not God's. Women and children should try to flee such situations, and pastors and elders should seek to help them out of, and keep them out of, such homes. But if homelife is safe, submission can still be extended during moments when a spouse is sane or sober. At other times, honoring the Lord and caring for oneself, one's family, and even one's neighbors, may very well have to be done against the wishes of a husband.

As noted above, sometimes trouble with submission is not just with the husband but also with the wife. Sometimes a wife will not want to submit to her husband, even in the best of situations. Emily sometimes crosses the line from constructive disagreement to a failure to submit, and she apologizes for it. She also seeks to remember that God promises to bless his own plans and not ours. It is his plan for there to be order in a marriage. It is best for you, and for yours, to follow this pattern and seek his blessing. We must believe this for God's honor and our good.

Some interpreters and translators of the Bible suggest that a wife's resistance to submission will be her lifelong struggle (see Gen. 3:16). Some husbands and even wives think that increased submission is always the key to a better marriage. But where relationship dynamics are always understood in terms of submission, we have oversimplified the callings of married couples, and it rarely plays out well. On the one hand, husbands or wives who think that every marital problem has to do with submission are oversimplifying in a way similar to dads and moms who think that every parenting problem boils down to one of disrespect. On the other hand, if a husband does see his spouse struggle with submission, his lifelong pursuit should be to sweeten what is bitter. A loving marriage sees work for oneself more quickly than work for one's spouse.

God tells us our roles. Our job is to keep picturing these roles in the best light. In a fallen world, we should expect that the best that God has designed for us will often be given a negative spin by non-Christians. Our culture offers Christian women little or no support in submission. This world will focus only on what it thinks a submissive wife *cannot* do.

This might have been amusing for William Gouge's own wife, Elizabeth. Elizabeth exercised hospitality on a large scale every Sunday as a support to her neighbors but also to her husband's ministry. In addition to running the household and its finances, she also had a quarterly allowance of money that she could spend without discussing it with her husband, and she spent most of it helping her neighbors. She was also careful to try to set an example of godliness in her own home as the principal leader under her husband; she attended lectures on the Bible during the week, and she participated in family devotions daily. As if that were not enough, she led her children and servants in a separate time of devotions each day as well. She had her own time of personal devotions and wrote prayers and spiritual guidebooks for other people. She studied the Scriptures so that she could answer any questions in biblical history or theology that might be put to her, and she spent as much time as possible reading theology and building her own theological library.

Because of the opposition of the world to submission, we have all the more reason to think through carefully why God's call for a wife to submit and to be husband-focused is in fact the best thing for us. So ultimately, what does it help us to see?

In our own home, and among other things, submission helps Emily to remember that in a perfect world Eve was created as

Adam's helper and that the role of helper, rather than leader, is not in itself demeaning. We also know this because God himself condescends to call himself our helper, and he is not demeaning himself when he does so. Jesus explained to his friends that he came to serve, and not to be served. Or take a theme from the apostle Paul: he calls us to comfort others with the comfort we've received (2 Cor. 1:3–4). We help others, remembering the help we receive.

Most of all we must focus on a strong relationship with our Lord. As we have our eye on what pleases him, we find that submission to such a Savior sweetens and enriches every other Christian responsibility and our perspective on all that we do.

Men and Marriage

RECOMMENDED READING

EPHESIANS 5:25–33

Ephesians 5 presents the bottom line for marriage by drawing parallel lines between Christian spouses and Christ and his church. That is easy to see. But have you ever noticed that after addressing wives in Ephesians 5, the apostle spends triple the amount of time addressing husbands? And have you ever wondered why?

As We Have Been Loved

For what it is worth, the puzzle of why Paul focuses mostly on men in marriage seems more of a husband question than a wife question. To most Christian women, that answer seems obvious: the Scriptures give husbands more instruction just because they need it. But perhaps the duties of husbands are discussed at such length because, in searching for an analogy of the love that husbands ought to have, Paul found space to talk about the love that Christ does have.

When the apostle switched sides in his analogy from wives and the church to husbands and Christ, he could not help but preach the Christian gospel. As one unmarried church father explained to his congregation, to grasp the measure of Christian submission and respect in marriage we must "hear also the measure of love."[8] Staggeringly, the measure of love presented to husbands is that shown by Jesus himself: "Husbands, love your wives," we are told, "as Christ loved the church" (Eph. 5:25).

We know that this is astonishing love because the Bible is clear about the love of Christ and what it looks like. He loves deeply: the Son of God gave himself up; he clung to no honor or privilege for himself. He loves sacrificially: Jesus gave himself up for his church; he offered his life for her life; he endured shame and scorn and mockery for another. He loves purposefully: Jesus wanted a splendid bride, an elect body of his own choosing. He loves faithfully: at the very least, Ephesians 5:26 reminds us that Christ's bride needed to be sanctified and cleansed; our Lord did not come to one who was beautiful but to one who needed to *become* beautiful, and he stays with her throughout that process.

We hear all this, and then we are told in 5:28 that "in the same way" husbands are to love their own wives. What a calling! In some way, husbands are to love their wives in a Christlike way and to help promote the purposes of Christ, in a Christlike fashion, for the good of their own wives. The love of Christ for his bride—a bride made up of sinful men and women—offers the model disposition that a husband ought to have for his wife, the orientation that should inform all of his thoughts, words, and actions.

Of course those comments need more comment. At their most unimaginative moments, husbands try to help spouses be like Christ's perfected bride by identifying their wives' faults with clinical precision. But if a husband wants to help his wife, it is better for him to ask himself some diagnostic questions:

1. Are you loving her with all that you are and all that you have? In other words, do you, like Christ, love your wife deeply, sacrificially, purposefully, and faithfully?
2. Are you praying for her and studying your spouse so that you can pray for her better?
3. What is your aim in your prayers? Is your prayer really for her? Or for you? What answers to your prayers can be seen?
4. Are you leading devotions that profit her? Are you trying to study the Bible and Christian doctrine so that what you say will be thoughtful and useful?
5. Does she know that you love her? Or does every moment with you feel like a teaching or improving moment for her?
6. Do you ensure that she has time to study God's word herself or with friends?

To pray and plan these sorts of things, and so much more, we need to be willing to let go of many other things that we ourselves hold dear; we need to let go of anything that could keep us from holding on to a spouse as we should. That is how Christ loved the church.

A Sanctified Wife

Husbands are to love as Christ loved the church. And one goal in this love is growth in holiness. Husbands, like Christ, are to care about sanctification. We are probably supposed to have figured this out simply because Ephesians 5 says the bride is like the church.

You may remember that the Old Testament calls God's people God's "bride." In this we see God's love for Israel, but we also recall that Israel was often his unfaithful spouse. The fact that a spouse may need help, may need change, and may need to repent is not a reason to stop loving. It is the reason for a husband to give his whole self to her, for that is how Christ loved the church.

So if we saved sinners are to love as Christ loved the church, we must pray for grace to love thoughtfully, humbly, with all that we have and all that we are. If we are to love as Christ loved the church, we are to give ourselves to our wives even when they are in need of sanctification; even when their words and actions are tarnished and marred.

Too often husbands are tempted to think that a monologue, a shake of the head, even a glare or an angry word is what they need to pass on to their spouse after she sins, especially if she sins against him. In our marriage, Emily has informed Chad that this is less of a blessing than he thinks. He has noticed that his negative signals do not make her task of respecting him any easier. We are to persuade our spouse with love. Christ did not demand that his church make herself beautiful. He worked to make her beautiful. Again, that is how Christ loved his bride.

To state the obvious, husbands cannot sanctify their wives. But as husbands intentionally seek the good of their spouses, in love, they should especially seek the great good of growth in grace. Husbands can be used as tools in Christ's workshop as he fashions and molds their wives alongside them.

Just as importantly, husbands can direct their wives to *God's* tools. Christ sanctified his church—he provided his word to change us; he provided washing with water to picture the washing away of our sins. A Christian husband can encourage his wife to make full use of the means of grace. He can pray and think and work toward her sanctification. Nothing less than this should be the goal. It is true that Paul offers only an analogy here when he speaks about a relationship between a husband and his wife and the relationship between Christ and the church. But it is the best analogy for marriage that this age has to offer, and we need to learn all that we can from it.

Brothers, do you want your wife to love you and respect you? Then respect her too, not reminding her of her own duties, but making her calling as easy as possible in a spirit of mutual submission and esteem.

Do you want to make it easier for your wife to love you and respect you? Don't shout and complain and excuse your sin. Be men who admit your wrongs and model the gospel.

Do you want your wife to love you and respect you? Then love her as Christ loved the church. Be willing to sacrifice your own ambitions and plans for her—even your own life.

Maybe that sounds too dramatic. How can you "give your life" unless war breaks out or a burglar breaks in? Perhaps you can give her your life by wearing yourself out in service to her instead of watching her wear out in service to you. Maybe you will get up and serve her when she is tired. Maybe you will mobilize (or immobilize!) the children and give her an evening with friends or a rest in bed. Maybe you will finish cleaning the house because her work was too much or because you want it tidy for guests and she has enough to do already.

Emily thinks it is worth Chad risking a personal example here. He tries to help her by protecting and promoting four features in her life: regular Bible study, exercise, sufficient sleep, and an understanding husband. This is no magic formula. The last one is the biggest wild card. And it took him years to find out that there were these four main ingredients that would help maximize her sanity and minimize her sin. But it is one example of the kind of thing that can prove very important in a marriage. What might it be in your marriage? Or in the marriage of a friend who needs your help?

Husbands, do you want your wife to love and respect you? Then help her to grow in holiness. And when your bride is radiant, or even when she is not, so love her that she will somehow grow even more in her radiance and inward beauty. Love and honor your wife like this, and it will make it easier for her to love and honor you.

I hope it is obvious by this point that a proper reading of Ephesians 5:25–33 reveals love to be more than a mere duty. It is not just one task that he does. No, love refers to a calling, a perspective, an orientation that characterizes how he does everything that he does.

As We Love Ourselves

We are to love as Christ loved the church. But maybe because we have a hard time processing something so divine, Scripture also supplies another analogy, this one very human. Ephesians 5:28 also tells husbands to love their wives as they love themselves—something that they tend to be fairly good at (often with a gadget or book in one hand and a beverage in the other). Literally, Paul says husbands are to love their wives like their own flesh, a sort of play on words, since he later alludes to the fact that husband and wife are called "one flesh" in Genesis 2.

Here's the point: if you are a married man, love your wife like you love yourself—and then some. Speak gently and make your words soft and tender, always remembering that you may need to eat them. And guard your time. You know how absorbing your work can be. Do enough work so that you can feed your wife and family. Do not do so much work that you cannot care for them in all the other ways they need. Protect your wife; comfort her and encourage her. Pray for her and with her daily, and you will have a stronger marriage.

Husbands are to love their wives as they love themselves, which is rarely anything but all consuming. Of course there are some people who do not take care of themselves. Paul speaks here in Ephesians 5 of healthy people as he teaches here about healthy marriages.

But, in fact, we take care of ourselves when we are not healthy, perhaps especially in such circumstances. What should you do when you notice something unhealthy in a spouse? Something problematic that cannot be hidden? Well, what would you do if this was true of your own self?

When he was preaching on this passage in the city of Antioch, John Chrysostom reminded his hearers just what we do when our body needs help. We nurture the defective, the lame, and the ailing parts of our bodies. We don't cut off an injured leg. We favor it; we nurse it back to normal. If husbands are to love their wives as their own body, they should do nothing less than this for them.

Sometimes when husbands see that something is broken, they rush to a diagnosis and to a cure. They too often think that they've understood everything on the spot. In their minds they're the clever detective, sizing up the situation in a flash and knowing exactly where they need to go next. In reality they're the doctor who half-listens to a complaint and then tells the patient to take two pills and call again in the morning. This is not what husbands want for themselves, and their wives don't want it either. Husbands need to seek understanding and, as God gives them insight, help their loved one to understand her own heart—the real cause of everyone's spiritual sickness.

Some men live like it is their main mission in life to teach their wife how to respect them. It is true that a husband may need to turn to the Scriptures and address this topic. But if submission is a problem, the answer is not found in crowding her. Give your spouse some room to get there; allow space for her to fail and learn along the way. This is what you would want for yourself. This is how you would love yourself if you could, and you are thankful that the Lord is gracious and patient with you as you grow in grace.

This kind of leadership and love and self-control is hard work, and we often lose patience when sinful patterns belong to someone other than ourselves. Perhaps that is why at the end of the conversation with husbands, Paul returns once more to the relationship between Christ and the church. In giving himself up for us, Jesus Christ was just taking care of his own body. He was nourishing and caring for that which was his. That is how a husband is to view and care for his own wife.

Created to Love

So husbands have been told that they are to love as Christ has loved the church. They are to love as they love their own selves. In the third place, husbands are to love their wives because that is what they were created to do.

When God presented Adam with Eve, he did not explain to the first man that from henceforth a man shall leave his father and mother because two can live cheaper than one. Husbands are to leave in order to cleave. They are to leave their parents in order to hold fast to another, to become one flesh.

Husbands are reminded here that a chief purpose of their marriage is to hold on to their wives, keeping them. In many marriages, the husband has forgotten this. Yes, some men are obsessive and jealous; they are controlling, fearful, and foolish. But too many husbands have let their wives go too easily, paying little attention to them, or are even willing to do without them or hoping to get someone better. Husbands need to cling to the gift that God has given them in their wives. They need to hold on to them with all their strength, remembering that they were created to love God, in part, by loving his gift to them in a wife.

We think Paul also reminds us of the book of Genesis to show us that in a very real way, God does consider husband and wife "one flesh." It's a topic to which we'll return. Here it is enough to remember that from the beginning, husbands were created to love their wives as their own bodies and as Christ loved his own body, the church.

The Mystery and the Majesty

Husbands are to love as Christ loved his church. Each Christian husband is to love his wife as he loves his own body. They are one. This unity between a man and a woman is expressed as something marvelous in the book of Proverbs. It is celebrated in the Song of Solomon.

The union that Paul is thinking about in Ephesians 5 is mysterious, but his thoughts—which have been drifting between the relationship of husband and wife and the relationship of Savior and believers—return one more time to Christ and the church.

You see, it was never possible for Jesus to serve as a mere illustration for Paul. There is much that is good, true, and beautiful about the analogy that Paul provides. But ultimately it is not the husband's duty to love his wife that Paul finds so profound. The mystery is that Christian marriage is given the honor of illustrating the gospel itself. What guilty person separated from God could have ever hoped that the Son of God would become a human being for our sake? What offender awaiting judgment and death could have ever dreamed that another would shed his blood in his place? How many who have a real sense of how awful we are truly think we can lose our guilty stains?

The mystery is that somehow God loves us and sent his Son for us. The almost bewildering fact is that Christ loved the church and gave himself up for her. And in that church are losers and failures of all sorts, including husbands.

There are homes where there has been far too little love. There are men who awake one day to see that they have shown their wives impatience and harshness when they should have held onto their wives, comforting instead of judging, loving their wives even half as much as they loved themselves. There are dying husbands who finally realize that with their foul tempers and impatience they have stolen years of joy from their wives. But thank God there is such a thing as redeeming love, and it is not too late to learn what it is about.

Perhaps you are a husband whose sin is now before you. What should you do? Certainly you should repent. Certainly you should ask forgiveness, humbly. But do not just say you are sorry.

Say what it is that you have done.

Use scriptural labels, rather than the sanitized labels of our culture, to describe that sin. Not, "Sorry, I was grouchy." But, "Please forgive me, I was selfish and impatient."

Say it in detail.

Say what you should have done instead.

Admit the damage you have done and the hurt you have caused. And say what you resolve to do now by God's grace.

And if you've sinned in front of others, repent in front of them too, even if it was in front of your friends and especially if your sin was before your children.

And be patient in awaiting forgiveness! We are not saying words in order to get something back in return.

Then when Satan resurrects old sins so that they can point a finger at you, remember God's power to save. Sing of that sacrificial love, not the one you failed to show but the love of Christ who saw the church—as it really is—and gave himself up for her. For that love will never lose its power till all the ransomed church of God be saved to sin no more. This is the profound mystery. It is also the majesty and the glory of the gospel.

Love and Respect

Paul closes with two brief summary statements. First to husbands: "Let each one of you love his wife as himself"; and to wives: "Let the wife see that she respects her husband" (Eph. 5:33). Here we are reminded that if a husband must so love his wife, then she must seek to make that task joyful and as easy as possible. One reason that she will show respect is to make it easy for him to love.

It is this mutual love and respect that is the secret to a happy marriage. Would it not be wonderful if Christian couples did not keep this secret to themselves but announced it in the way in which they live? Let it be the prayer of every Christian person reading this book that the marriages in their church will serve as a wonderful picture of the gospel, and that this gospel will be the most important thing in our marriages.

But with the Holy Spirit's help, let us never forget that each of us is marrying a sinner and not a savior. The reality of the gospel will always be the best model for marriage, but your marriage may often fail to be a good model of the gospel. You will face moments, and perhaps even seasons, when affection and respect will not be what they should be, when saints are not loving and sinners need more grace.

So let us keep before us the love that Christ has for his church. He did not pursue those who were always warm and kind; rather, he followed after those who turned their backs on him. He did not come to those who were already righteous but to those who dared to insult him or ignore him. In short, Christ came to save sinners, and that is what we are, even in marriage. Perhaps especially in marriage. He lost his life so that we could find forgiveness. Of course, we are speaking to all of us here, because we are speaking of Christ and his church.

Winning in Marriage

RECOMMENDED READING

I PETER 3:1–7

In reflecting on the duties of husbands and wives, we've been considering ways in which marriages can get better. But we live in a world where things are broken, including marriages. So what are we to do with marriages that get worse?

Thankfully the Bible discusses not just ideal relationships, but real ones. In fact, the apostle Peter deals directly with the topic of marital tensions, those caused by sin and those sparked by weakness. For that reason we need this chapter, for we need to know how to win when an argument comes up.

What Did Jesus Do?

The clue for what to do comes at the end of 1 Peter 2. Before discussing homelife, Peter discusses the workplace. And he notes that while people can be good and gentle; they can also be unjust. So what are Christians to do? The apostle's first response is to point us to the suffering Savior. Peter does not ask, *What would Jesus do?* but *What did Jesus do?* And the answer is this:

[Jesus] committed no sin, neither was deceit found in his mouth. When he was reviled, he did not revile in return; when he suffered, he did not threaten, but continued entrusting himself to him who judges justly. (1 Pet. 2:22–23)

Jesus was our substitute. He took our place. But he was also showing us what it means to entrust ourselves to the one who judges justly.

This may not seem to be a winning strategy, but the word of God says it is. That means that we do not retaliate. God will either judge the unjust for their wrongs, or he will show them their sin and lead them to the cross, where sin has been judged in the sin-bearer, Jesus. That means that in the midst of injustice, we entrust ourselves to God. If we are falsely accused or poorly treated, we remember that our hope and strength and song is found in Christ alone. Who is he that condemns us? In Christ we are justified.

In the injustice of the workplace Peter points us to Jesus. He then turns to the topic of marriage, making the connection with the word *likewise* (1 Pet. 3:1). He uses this word because both at work and at home, people can be unfair. But he also uses that word because we are to respond in the same way for the same reasons, following and trusting the same Savior.

Relationships are not supposed to slide downward, but we all know that there are marriages in which spouses are not believing the word of God or are not living in faithful obedience. Peter addresses this scenario first by addressing the matter of problematic husbands: men who act like bad employers, making unreasonable demands while making end runs around responsibilities.

It is worth saying that the very fact that Peter was willing to raise this topic ran counter to polite pagan society. Good Greeks and Romans taught that a woman was supposed to follow her husband no matter what. A woman was devious and destabilizing if she had a mind of her own. Peter, on the other hand, calls for women in hard situations to try to win over their husbands. For a Christian, it is a matter of real concern if a marriage has spiraled into cold war or pitched battles, or if a woman's husband does not honor the Scriptures.

Women: Winning without Words

If you were accosted with the trailer for the 2006 movie *The Break-Up*, you'll have seen in two minutes the three steps that people take to restore a struggling marriage: they fight (as if that helps), they try to make the other partner jealous (as if that can't go wrong), and they try to make themselves more visually attractive.[9]

In these opening verses Peter reveals a different recipe for overcoming conflict, and it contains a couple of key ingredients. Along the way Peter deals with fighting in verses 1–2 when he talks about winning without words. He quickly crosses out the possibility of flirting in verse 2 when he calls for purity. And in verses 3–6 he addresses the desire to make oneself more attractive.

The first counsel that Peter prescribes is that a Christian woman should seek to win her husband without words. When a romantic man turns out to be an unhelpful or even a hurtful husband, a wife is often strongly tempted to hit back. She goes on strike or works to rule. At the very least, favors and privileges are withheld, and the spouse is made to know why. It is in this context that words become frozen and few or heated and many, for it is easy to turn to lecturing amidst legitimate disappointments and irritations.

Peter calls wives in this situation to try a different path: to gain their husbands by what they do instead of what they say. Notice that he is not saying that she must never speak to him about the danger of sin and the hope of rescue in Christ. But he is saying that the chief instrument in bringing husbands onboard is not the words they hear but the actions and attitudes they see. Conduct is king, or queen.

Sometimes in a difficult marriage one or both partners wants to fight. At other times, a spouse drifts away or plunges into impurity. In these situations the wounded person might flirt with someone outside the marriage. He or she may begin to focus on other people at the gym, at work, or onscreen either as a way of revenge or with the thought that the wandering spouse may become jealous in some helpful way. Sometimes spouses are simply careless of whether all this might lead to distance, separation, and divorce.

Unfaithfulness as a form of attack or of self-defense is ungodly and corrosive to a marriage. And Peter, at the end of 3:2, addresses this kind of tactic in a marriage and tells us that even if some husbands do not obey the word, their wives must not only remain respectful but remain pure. Faithfulness to Christ requires that we not fantasize about another person or a different marriage.

Husbands can be won without words and by persistently pure and respectful conduct. They can also be attracted by real beauty. It is an ageless practice to deal with the inward pain of rejection by attempting to make ourselves more attractive on the outside. Peter mentions the usual three devices: hair, jewelry, and clothing. Today we've invented a few more. But the problem is that we chronically address the outside of the person rather than the inside.

Christians have parked at the curb of 1 Peter 3:3 for centuries to complain about immodest or expensive outfits. Nonetheless, that is not the apostle's point here. Peter is simply saying that the deepest beauty is not external. The truly captivating woman has adorned the hidden person of the heart—the inner self. A woman's character cannot be enhanced by cutting her hair, changing her earrings, or shortening her dress. It can be enhanced and evidenced in her actions and words.

Perhaps you are a wife, or know a wife, who has a husband who has drifted from God or from the standards in God's word or from a marriage. God's word calls a woman in such a situation to go for the imperishable good looks of a gentle, humble, considerate, and quiet spirit. Do you know a friend in this situation? Encourage her to adopt this passage as her own.

Not only is this best for your marriage; it is of great worth in God's sight. It is precious, and every Christian knows why. God esteems this kind of loveliness because it can exist only where there is a true and steady trust in Christ. God prizes this kind of costly, expensive beauty because it was purchased at the price of his own Son. If you know a husband who does not obey the word, he needs to be rescued in just the same way that you were: by the Lord Jesus Christ. Nice hair and good clothes may win a battle, but it will never win the war.

Your husband needs the one who wore the crown of thorns, who had his clothing bartered away so he could take the shame and penalty of sin. He is the one whom we must trust to repair our marriages, one heart at a time. So why does Peter call wives to an inner beauty? Because it is this that will make a husband look at you in a new way. A husband will ask what has happened. And he will be told about Jesus.

Peter doesn't say it in so many words, but a woman who believes this truth will have a loveliness of her own. It will be seen in her spirit. This kind of deep attractiveness can increase in sickness. It can flourish even as the marks of weary Christian service are evidenced on our bodies. These good looks can actually increase in age, and Peter turns to the winner of the Miss Patriarch contest to make that point.

Abraham's wife Sarah is an interesting case. Genesis 12 tells us that she remained an incredibly attractive woman until late in life, but Abraham did not appreciate her as he should have. While he is a father in the faith, he was not much of a husband. Twice he gave Sarah up to another man rather than risk danger to himself. Nonetheless, she still chose to follow the maximal form of respect in the culture of her day, even calling Abraham "lord," or "master."[10] Peter's point is that in spite of her famous beauty, the most beautiful feature the Lord saw in her was her character.

What about Fear and Intimidation?

Peter concludes his instructions to wives by saying that you are Sarah's children if you do what is right, and if you do not live in fear and intimidation.

It is easy for a husband at his worst moments to intimidate his wife with his louder voice or his bigger build; Christian men must always be very careful here. But many women can also testify that it is scary to watch a spouse whom they love step off the path that leads to life. It is a fearful fact that men who turn from the

Lord can become bad company. Wives not only ask "What will happen to him?" Some will also ask, "What will happen to me?" Will he come home with kind words or cutting ones? What will today be like?" And for some, this is the question of *every* day. Here too we need to live by faith rather than by fear, and what this looks like will depend on each situation.

If he has so deserted his wife and family that he abuses them instead of helping them, then they need to seek refuge somewhere else. Abusive people must repent of their sins and turn to Christ, but our belief in the message of the gospel does not mean that the Christian family, or the Christian church, needs to be a safe haven for abusers. If people in a dangerous situation flee, they do so not only to save themselves or their children but also because they have in some sense already been deserted by their spouse.

But often an ungodly husband does not make his wife's life dangerous; he is content to make it miserable. Augustine of Hippo had a father like that. Patricius swung wildly from exceptional kindness to an exceptionally quick temper. The saving grace in the family was lived out by Augustine's mother, Monica, who managed to honor her husband, making it easy for him to love her, in spite of his faults. She also taught other women to do the same with their husbands. Her husband first came to love, respect, and then admire her. He also came to Christ. I should note that the lessons that Scripture teaches here are useful not only for marriages in which a man is thoroughly disobedient to God but also for marriages in which men are occasionally disobedient.

So no matter what challenges we may face, we must pray that we will continue to follow the sure counsel of Scripture, even when the going is hard and long. Too often we say, "I tried that. Now

I want to try something else." This is understandable. But there is no plan B. There is only Peter's plan A. And there is a reason for this. Peter issues the calling of Christians to suffer graciously not because it always has the desired effects—not because it always works—but because it glorifies God. And that is always a win in marriage.

Husbands Honoring Wives

Having said so much to wives in conflict, the Bible also has something to say to husbands. That is why Peter begins 1 Peter 3:7 by again writing, "Likewise . . . ," or "In the same way . . ." This connects Peter's instruction to the previous paragraph (3:1–6), and probably to the paragraph on problems in the workplace (2:18–25).

The Holy Spirit draws a connection here, but there is also a contrast. A husband may have a difficult wife and may need to take a healthy dose of Peter's counsel for himself. But here Scripture talks not about a wife's potential faults but about her weakness.

We live at a time that does not really know how to deal with weakness. This is a dog-eat-dog world. What time do we really have for those who are weak? Because we think only the fittest survive, some people try to bury their own weakness, hiding or denying their limitations or frailties. We see this in dysfunctional marriages. Other people try to defend the weak by denying reality; they paper over the facts and assure us that women and men are the same in all their strengths. We see this in our culture's gender wars.

Some among us hide or deny weakness. Others take advantage of it. Sadly, we've all seen men who intimidate, humiliate, neglect, control, and criticize their wives because of what they see as weakness. Peter calls husbands in particular to honor their wives in their weakness. So let us comment on what that weakness might be, how a husband should treat his wife, and why.

What?

Scholars offer more than one option of what this weakness in 1 Peter 3:7 could be. One perspective studies the word that Peter uses when he refers to "the woman," which is plausibly translated "the one who is feminine." According to this perspective, the feminine one is a weaker vessel because she shows a wider range of emotions and consistently loses in arm-wrestling contests. A husband is not to take advantage of her feminine characteristics, not least when it comes to his businesslike approach to problems or his physical power. Alternatively, Peter may have in mind a perception of weakness arising from the wife's position as one who is not the higher authority in the home. She is weaker in that that he is the head and she is not.

Of course, whatever the definition of weakness we might use, we are not denying that women have many different important strengths where men have profound weaknesses. Nor should we pass over the reality that women are called to great strength of character in the previous verses. And to speak of a woman's comparative strength is to say nothing about her physical endurance. To choose only the most obvious example, women endure pain in childbirth that makes a man shudder even to contemplate. Giving birth is still the gold standard for human toughness as well as human love. And yet let us own Scripture's message here: a wife has weaknesses unique to who she is, and eventually even the thickest husband will catch on to this. When he does, he is to prize her for everything that she is and not despise her for anything she is not.

Whatever the precise definition of weakness, a husband's responsibility is clear. Husbands are to prize, to treasure, to value their wives, not just because they are people but because they are women. And there is a public aspect to honor, for it is very important how she is presented and discussed before others. A friend of ours took this fact about homelife into his workplace and made it clear to his male colleagues that there would be no negative comments about their wives. He insisted that they honor their spouses or not talk about them at all.

A woman is a wonderful gift to a man. This is obvious for those with eyes to see, and yet a husband can sometimes find it hard to value his wife as a woman if she slows him down, processes problems differently, or offers distinct perspectives. So what are men tempted to do? They are tempted to push, to put down, to ignore. They are tempted to dishonor their wives, taking advantage of the ways in which they are weaker vessels, or simply different.

Consider how often men are critical because they think they could have done something better than their wives. The truth, Chad says, is that we men are often wrong, and we'd botch the job entirely. But even if we are right, we're *behaving* wrongly. Elsewhere men are called to love their wives. Here men are told to actually honor them. Peter very deliberately shuts off men's usual escape routes when he calls them to honorable living.

How?

So how is a husband to deal with any perceived weakness in a wife? The first thing that Peter calls men to do is to live with their wives "with understanding" or "in an understanding way" (1 Pet. 3:7).

This could mean that he is to live with an understanding of all that God calls him to be and do; in this context, he would be called to understand, among other things, what God requires of him with respect to his wife. Alternatively, Peter could mean that a husband is to live with understanding of his wife in particular; husbands are to live with real consideration, a considerate life that is characterized by knowledge.

Either way, for the purpose of better honoring her and making her duties easier, a husband is to learn his wife's strengths and weaknesses, her likes and dislikes, her fears and insecurities. His privileged information about his God-given responsibilities and his knowledge of his wife is not to be used against her but for her.

Although husbands sometimes forget, living with a woman is not like rooming with a man. It takes minimal effort for men to understand each other. Television plus food offers a fairly predictable formula for male happiness. Experience tells most of us that it is possible to live with a roommate for a long time and acquire very little wisdom about relationships, in part because buddies can be replaced in ways that wives cannot.

Living with a wife requires real thoughtfulness, some of which comes only from on-the-job training. For those who have tried to understand their wives, many can testify that they found the learning curve steep, almost vertical, and devoid of plateaus. Learning the other sex is complicated, and it takes honest work.

It doesn't help that both men and women think that their needs are fairly obvious and that their communications are usually clear. But the main challenge is not only with the lines of communication in a marriage, but with the kind of content, or lack thereof, being communicated.

A subset of the times that Chad sins against Emily, he has a sense that there is much more to the problem than he even realizes. On some of these occasions he has had to say, "Emily, I'm sure that this should be obvious, and I'm sorry that I have to ask, but I am so lost that I'm not really sure what I should say here. Tell me what I should say, not so that I can avoid thinking for myself, but so that I can learn to understand you and what I should be seeing in this situation." Thankfully, she is graciously committed to making his job as a husband easier. She sees that this kind of exchange is a win in marriage, much better than trading defensive comments or offensive evaluations—something we also sometimes do.

Peter calls husbands to live with their wives in an understanding way. This is closely tied to his second *how* comment in verse 7: he needs to live with her in such a way that he is showing her honor. A man honors his wife by respecting her, listening to her, maintaining her authority before others in the home, protecting her from harm, upholding her good name, supporting her financially, and placing a proper trust and confidence in her. A man honors his wife as he prizes her counsel and seeks her correction.

Perhaps there are better ways to communicate the idea of honor, but the real surprise is that husbands are called to honor their partners at all.

Peter earlier summed up the duty of Christian citizens by telling them to honor the emperor. Here he sums up the duty of Christian husbands by telling them to honor their wives. Now there is surely a difference in the way in which a man honors the emperor and the way in which a man honors his wife. But there is a sense in which a man is to roll out the red carpet for the woman in his life. If a man's home is his castle, his wife should be its queen.

Peter's word choice, *honor*, can hardly have been more elevated—which is a good thing to remember after what he said in verses 1–6. If anyone complains that in her calling as a wife, she is reduced to a servant by verses 1–6, we also need to complain that she is elevated to a princess by verse 7. Scripture is not privileging one party in the marriage over another.

Chad did not always get this emphasis on honor, and it was only in writing the final draft of this book that he admitted to Emily that he went to two different friends to complain about her, once in the first year of their marriage and again five years later. These men proved true friends to *both* of us. They said no. Willing to embarrass Chad by shutting him down—firmly—they explained that they were not going to listen to him vent about Emily, and they gave reasons why. One of these brothers was married, the other not, but both of them understood more clearly than Chad in that moment that it was his calling to uphold and honor his wonderful, even if imperfect, wife.[11]

Why?

Peter ends his thoughts on marriage by offering two reasons *why* a husband must understand and honor his wife. The first is found once again in the idea of mutuality: husbands are to honor their wives as if they were coheirs of a life of grace—because in fact they are.

It used to be that women were only heirs if specific provision was made or if no sons in a family survived. In some parts of the world this is still the case. But that is not the Lord's model for his people. Christian sisters have the same position as Christian brothers. We are all heirs of an eternal life of grace, and we are already living off the proceeds of what God has put in trust for us.

Our names are written into the will of God together, and together we inherit all that Christ has earned and purchased on our behalf. Surely this ought to help us esteem every Christian with the respect he or she deserves. It is to teach us to respect others that Peter brings this inheritance to our attention. Every person who truly trusts in Christ, however muddled in however many ways, remains a coheir with us of every treasure of grace.

If grace is to be our guiding light for every Christian relation, then this is all the more true for Christian marriage. A man can honor his wife because she is the joy of his life, the beauty of his dreams, and the best friend he has ever had. But a Christian man honors his wife not because she is so worthy in herself, but because God has declared her worthy of honor in giving his only Son for her life.

For that matter, the same truth drives in both directions: a husband does not earn the full measure of respect that his wife is to grant him. No, it is by grace that he is declared worthy of any respect at all, by the one who redeemed him.

Even Hillary of Arles, a fifth-century, semi-Pelagian bishop who was wrong in most things that mattered, was able to see that "both parties are heirs of eternal life which God gives by grace, not by any merit which we may possess, and we do well to remember that 'it depends not on man's will or exertion, but on God's mercy.'"[12] If a Pelagian can see the primary importance of God's grace in marriage, how much more should a good Augustinian?

Do you want to help a Christian spouse through this life and into the next? Tell her who she is: a coheir of the grace of life; a person saved by the mercy and love of God; someone kept by his faithfulness and not her own energetic holiness. Tell him that you *are* no better and *deserve* no better; you too are an heir of heaven not by right, but by grace. Tell him when he sins against you that you are happy to forgive him because you also have been forgiven. Tell her that you love her despite her failings, because, like her, you know what it is to fail, but also what it is to be rescued by the God of grace. Tell him that whatever the Lord will bring his way in this life, he will not be alone but is part of a vast family won by the undeserved mercy of a holy God. Tell the truth, and the truth will set both of you free.

The final reason why husbands should honor their wives has to do with prayer. We don't talk about it often, but it is possible for our Father in heaven to have little interest in a man's prayers, for Peter says, "Likewise, husbands, live with your wives in an understanding way . . . so that your prayers may not be hindered" (1 Pet. 3:7). We don't like to think about it, but it is possible for our prayers to be hindered or detained. Heaven has a detainment center for the prayers of men who will not honor their wives.

Those who habitually and unrepentantly make no efforts to understand and honor their wives, those who abuse them for their weakness, those who refuse to obey the word—they should not expect to find God eager to hear their prayers. God knows the way in which husbands treat their wives in the privacy of their homes, and he has ways of dealing with them. He is not a helpless father, hoping you will treat his daughter well. He is a ferocious defender of all his children, including the child of God you married.

This is a solemn thought. We have all tasted the bitter cup of failure. None of us deserve God's mercy or answers to our prayers. But some of us have drunk deeply from the cup of careless, loveless treatment of our wives, the spouses whom God has given us.

In any case, we need to ask for mercy, for this is the one prayer God will always hear. High and mighty husbands need to bow before the throne of grace. They must cling to the one who was broken and bruised, the one who shed his atoning blood for their sakes. Anything less than this kind of prayer threatens our spiritual security.

We men, Chad says, are sometimes dishonest with ourselves and others. Let us be honest now. Some of us feel a distance, a spiritual coldness, a deadness in our bones. Heaven seems closed to us, and we wonder what is wrong. In situations like this, a Christian friend might ask if we are faithful in our quiet times. The word of God is asking if we are faithful to our spouse.

Scripture's teaching is challenging for all of us. Maybe you're a husband who has neither understood nor honored his wife. Or maybe you're a wife who has tried to win with words more than actions. Perhaps even now you are recalling your faults. With the assistance of the accuser, we walk through life with our own private movie theaters; our memories are box offices always offering posters and trailers that review our worst sins. Satan invites us to see replays of depression and discouragement, always hoping we'll finally sit down and take in full-feature films about our failures and foolishness. So what are we to do? Let us return once more to Peter's prefatory comments about Jesus:

If when you do good and suffer for it you endure, this is a gracious thing in the sight of God. For to this you have been called, because Christ also suffered for you, leaving you an example, so that you might follow in his steps. (1 Pet. 2:20–21)

Christ suffered for you as a substitute, and as an example. Let your spouse see Christ in your life, hear him in your encouragements, and find him in your prayers, and he or she may end up trusting in him. When it comes to dealing with marital sin or marital weakness, this is the only winning strategy.

Family and Marriage

There is a saying that people sometimes use when they want to be alone together: "Two's company, three's a crowd." So far in these lessons we've been talking about twosomes, but the reality is that marriages are often crowded. In fact, they are meant to be, for married couples live in community and usually have family. We connect to community through Christ (we'll talk about that in a later chapter). We connect to family by birth or adoption.

In the previous chapter we talked about sin and weakness in husbands and wives, following the focus of 1 Peter 3. There too we saw the usefulness of Ephesians 5:21 and the way of grace and love: if husbands are to understand and honor their wives, wives should endeavor to be understandable and honorable; if wives are to respect their husbands, husbands should seek to be respectable. In this chapter we build on that discussion, asking how, by grace, married couples can better serve their families.

Leaving Parents

There is no question that couples sometimes feel crowded, in the first place, because of their families of origin. You may remember that Ephesians 5 ends with an afterword that is forward looking: Paul reminds us that married people are starting a family. Something new is made because a husband and wife are now united.

This is exciting for the couple but often challenging for families, so preachers tell parents at a wedding that no one is losing anything; one side is gaining a son-in-law and the other a daughter-in-law. Nonetheless there is also a very real sense in which children are separating from father and mother and siblings. Honor and love and friendship continue, but a new alignment of affection and respect is created or affirmed.

In saying these kinds of things Ephesians 5 is clearly echoing Genesis 2, for when the Bible first summarizes what it means for a man and woman to be together, it mentions "leaving father and mother," and it mentions becoming one flesh. In the old King James Version these two activities are summed up as leaving and cleaving. It is not true of everyone, but many couples find that the cleaving-to-one-another part of marriage is easy, and the leaving-parents-and-family part of marriage is more complicated.

What cleaving looks like will, of course, depend on one's culture. For some cultures, with extended families living together, leaving means getting your own room. We'll go out on a limb and say that this level of leaving is not optimal in a marriage, even if it is sometimes necessary. But whatever the shape leaving might take, people experience the difficulty of leaving on a personal level. If you are used to spending a lot of time visiting with parents or were perhaps living with them, then not seeing them on a regular basis can create a void in your life. This is especially true where a spouse has been particularly close to a parent.

Yet if a husband is to be a one-woman man, it is hard to see how he can ordinarily spend an hour a day on the phone with his mother. A parallel point can be made for a wife and her parents. Sometimes parents invite their married children to join them on a vacation, perhaps offering to help with planning or paying costs. We have often gone on vacations with parents, but we pause to ask if we are enabling leaving and cleaving. If you are the Christian parent of married children, you will want to think through what you can do to best facilitate their duty to leave you and cleave to each other and not pressure them to spend time with you when it might be better for them to devote that time to each other. This is grace in action for our parents.

Leaving is hard for some married children. It is at least as hard for parents and often for a longer period of time. Married Christian couples need to care about that, because we want to make the duty of our parents to let go as easy as possible. Of course we will explain that travel and telephone time may need to be altered. But we will probably want to say more. We may acknowledge that a new marriage can leave holes in other lives. We may acknowledge a sense of loss or loneliness. And we may even talk about Augustine of Hippo or Jonathan Edwards.

If Augustine has taught the church anything, it is that every loss, and each experience of loneliness, contains its own lesson: human relations in this life cannot fully satisfy the sense of longing for relationship built into each one of us. There are things on this earth that are left broken in order to make us long for what is not. We need to preach this to one another.

Edwards is helpful here too. Near the end of his book *Charity and Its Fruits*, he has a chapter entitled "Heaven, a World of Love." Edwards points out that there is only one place where love faces no limitations. When we go to be with the Lord, love will not be hindered by distance, by a lack of time together, by an uneven return of love given to others, by a difference in possessions, by circumstances that dampen love, and by differing relations. There is a joy not experienced in marriages in the state of grace that will be experienced by people in the state of glory.

So far we have only mentioned the challenge of adult children leaving their parents. There is also the difficulty that comes when parents leave us. Even if you and your spouse think you have found the right formula for relating to parents, the formula might need to be adjusted when you lose a parent, and the surviving parent suddenly feels a bit like a dependent—or actually becomes one. Once again, in the midst of compassion and love, husbands and wives must remember that they cannot fill the void left by their parent's missing spouse.

Loving Parents

We have been talking about parental problems on a personal level. We can also discuss them on a relational level. In marriage, dynamics between spouses can often become particularly complicated when it comes to dealing with in-laws. Generalizations are always lobbying for exceptions, but in general, dealing with a new set of parents offers hilly terrain.

To put it another way, there is a reason why there is a whole genre of mother-in-law jokes, that go back almost as far as the genre of *joke* itself. There is the one about the guy who is told he has only six months to live. As soon as the doctor tells him the news, he turns to his wife and says, "We're moving in with your mother." When the doctor asks why, he explains, "A half a year with her will feel like forever." (We can only repeat the joke because we have wonderful in-laws!)

Sometimes we marry into whole families that are complicated. Sarah Edwards, Jonathan's wife, found herself grafted by marriage into a psychologically complicated family tree that was marred by an axe murderer. Sometimes a particular person stands out. When Chad's parents bought their first house, one of his grandmothers, a precious woman with strong convictions, didn't like their front porch. She said so. They didn't listen. The next thing they knew, she was taking a whack at it with an axe. And the thing is, it wasn't even her axe.

For most of us, in-law problems are more pedestrian and have nothing to do with axes. But these challenges can be equally dangerous because they are less obvious. Just think about the in-law challenges you might have experienced. It is not uncommon when spending time with your spouse's family to see not only their strengths but also their faults in a larger perspective.

There is the moment when you realize that your spouse's most irritating sin is typical of his or her entire family. There is the moment when out of habit they treat your spouse like their child, and you watch in horror as your spouse slips into the role of a dependent. There are the moments when parents try to shape your decisions by trying to win their child to their own point of view about finances, parenting, or decorating. This use of a relationship is a significant parental invasion, one that crosses a line and can threaten the unity of a marriage. When manipulation is at work, in-laws feel like outlaws.

Proverbs 19:11 reminds us that it is a "glory to overlook an offense," and we should allow as few things as possible to qualify as offenses. She should not take umbrage when he admires his mother's cooking. He should not be jealous if he doesn't get her family's jokes. And everyone should remember that unimportant issues are only amplified in families that are more dysfunctional, or when we see some relatives all the time, or when the only time that we see them is when we are thrown together in close quarters or for intense conversations.

A married couple who wants to help a spouse or parents to fulfill their duties will be aware of these dynamics, talk through them together, and then talk to parents too. Without this, leaving and cleaving will be hindered.

Honoring Parents

One text of Scripture that informs our relations with family is the command in Genesis 2 to leave and cleave. A second biblical duty helps us to navigate, even balance, these child-parent relations. It is the command to honor our parents (Deut. 5:16; Eph. 6:1).

Odd as it may sound, married couples must not obey their parents (Ex. 20:12). That would be to *not* leave a father and mother. For a married couple to simply obey his or her parents would be to miss the fact that something new is made in a marriage, including a new head of a new household.

That said, respect must continue. Honoring parents is not just for children. It is for adults too. So do you remember the respect you showed when you were dating or courting? Those conversations when you wanted your potential in-laws to like you? All that good behavior that was on display because you wanted your possible spouse to think that you respected your parents too? That must not be turned off because it is too inconvenient to continue or because the marriage deal is now sealed. Whatever the mixture of motivations for the burst of good behavior that often characterizes family relations during an engagement, it all trends in the right direction, even if the motivations for action need to be recalibrated.

Of course a married couple may do things differently in a marriage than their parents did in theirs. Yes, we cannot escape the fact that in some respects, we are made in the image of our parents. Yet while we consciously (or unconsciously) follow our parents in some areas, there will be places where we choose another path. Your parents never discussed finances; you do. Your parents always bought expensive items, assuming they would last; you don't. Your parents put too many kids into too small of a car for too long of a drive and called it a vacation; you plan a "staycation" and read a book.

We can do things differently, but we still must honor our parents in the way in which we relate to them. Even significant issues must be discussed with respect, even if—especially if—we know we won't agree.

Again, what that honor looks like will vary in its details, but the generalities will stay the same. We'll build up their names in public, guarding their reputations as best as we can. We'll keep our dirty laundry at home. As much as is right and safe, what happens in the family, stays in the family. We'll seriously consider their advice, even if we decide not to follow it. We'll persevere in communicating with them and try to assume the best of their motives, even in difficult relationships, because God in his providence put us in each other's life.

Again, the extent to which this may be possible depends in some degree on your family history. If a parent was abusive, you will do more protecting than communicating. If serial bankruptcies or gambling addictions run in the family, you may not want to consult a given parent for financial counsel.

It is because of our desire to honor parents that we try to pray in a focused way in the days leading up to a parental visit. It is because we honor them that we discuss issues directly rather than use a spouse as a go-between. And we expect the same of our parents.

The way in which we treat our parents throughout our marriage, from the complicated questions of the early days to our care of them at the end of their days, is a key part of our Christian testimony. Helping each other love and honor our parents, helping one another through thoughtful leaving and cleaving, rather than venting or complaining, is part of what goes into a godly marriage. And if this has not been a part of our pattern, if we have not helped our spouse or children honor our parents, we can repent and start anew or confess our sins and do a better job of honoring their memories.

Need we add that much of this applies equally to blended families? We may need to help a husband or wife through the challenges of being a stepparent. We may need to help a spouse help children to honor a biological parent who is now your spouse's ex-spouse. These are intricate dynamics, even further complicated by ex-in-laws and so on. But if by God's grace we respect and love one another, we will help our spouse in their effort to respect and love their family.

Being Parents

Marriage can be crowded by parents. As we've indicated, marriages are also crowded by children. Actually, when we read a command to honor parents, many married couples will not think of the honor we owe to our parents but the honor that our children owe to us.

We have found that the most difficult part of parenting is figuring out which faults in a child can be pinned on our parents and which should be blamed on each other. We prefer the first option and we are developing a theory to support it. Have you ever heard of the twins gene? The chance of a woman having twins is doubled if *her* mother was a twin; the pattern skips generations. We sort of hope sin is like this. It cannot be Emily's character faults showing up in our daughters—it must somehow be Emily's mother's character faults (an implausible idea, once one meets her mother)!

Let us be clear that this is not a parenting book. Our purpose here is not to give advice about parenting. But parenting is often a task of married people, so we want to think about parenting as it relates to marriage. It is a duty that usually accompanies marriage, so we want to think about it in that context.

First, we must remember that marriage has purposes independent of raising children, as we mentioned in the first chapter. Even if there is a sense in which we never stop being a parent, we must be clear that our marriage comes before our parenting. Indeed, it is good for our children to see this in the way in which we act and speak. It reflects creation priorities. Husband and wife existed before father and mother.

Thus parents would be wise to spend time alone, or time together, that children may not interrupt. For what it is worth, we established a practice of a Sunday night date. Since the children have a square meal after the morning worship service, we give them a quick "breakfast dinner" after the evening worship service, and then we—just the two of us, or perhaps the two of us with other adults—eat together after putting younger children to bed. We were also blessed with a wonderful friend in our congregation who knew how important it is for couples to spend time together. When we had not gone out together for many months, she finally took matters in hand. She approached us after a worship service, open planner or diary in hand, and asked if she could babysit for free on Tuesday or Thursday. If not then, when? She did not leave until all of us had an evening written down. And she did this many times. It doesn't matter how you carve out your time as a couple. Just find some way to express the priority of the marriage in the family, perhaps even asking the Lord and others for help.

Much more importantly, Christian couples should pray together and have times of worship as a couple and not simply as a family. Their life together as a couple must not get swallowed up by life together as a family. It is natural for parents to feel a sense of loss when their children leave home. There is a change of purpose when the last child gets married or, for that matter, is put on a bus for kindergarten or gets dropped off at college. But people with a child-centered marriage are the ones whose marriage struggles with an empty nest or who fail to allow their own children to leave and cleave if they in turn get married.

In marriage, we must train one another to love our children selflessly, but also to love our spouse selflessly. As we will see in the next chapter, 1 Corinthians 7 teaches us that we radically belong to one another. For all of the affection we must have for our children, the same cannot be said of the parent-child relationship. This is an important truth that we will also have to pass on to our children, especially as they get older.

Parenting can challenge a marriage in so many ways. Young couples are advised to begin reading about child-rearing before they have children, to read about discipline while their children are still learning to make eye contact, and to start reading about parenting teens when their children are not yet tweens. Presenting a united front and encouraging one another to stay the course is one of the ways in which we can bless one another in our marriage. Trying to parent together while parents disagree about parenting is very hard. It also makes it harder for our children to follow their calling of honoring their parents when fathers and mothers are not on the same page.

If we are to honor and respect one another, we must also learn to give way to one another, especially if we are losing our cool. Because we are to seek to make our children's duties easier, Ephesians 6:4 tells parents not to provoke or exasperate their children. Sometimes we don't see that we individually are doing this, but our spouse does. We should not disagree in front of our children, so if your spouse is sending you warning signs, honor him or her. Avoid disagreement by deferring to your spouse. We have sometimes failed to do this. We always regret it later.

To say this is to discuss the problem of sin. If we sin against your spouse—raising your voice, making an unkind comment, ignoring his or her wise counsel—whatever it might be, we must repent. And if that sin occurs before one or more children, or before our parents or friends, we must repent before them too. There have been far too many family devotions in our home that have begun with one or both parents having to confess that our actions or words were sinful before God and hurtful toward one another. But it would be much worse if there had been no confession at all, for children are imitators of their parents, including the marriage of their parents.

Imitating a Parent

We've spent a lot of time thinking about marriage at the end of Ephesians 5 and parenting in marriage at the beginning of Ephesians 6. But we'd be missing a great deal if we forgot what Paul said about forgiveness at the end of Ephesians 4 and imitation at the beginning of Ephesians 5.

Paul's closing point for sinners in chapter 4 calls them to "be kind to one another, tenderhearted, forgiving one another, as God in Christ forgave you" (v. 32). If we are able to show kindness and tenderheartedness in marriage, and our parents and children see it, we will be reflecting the character of a Christian's true Father. If our marriage is characterized by this kind of forgiveness, we will leave a legacy worthy of imitation for our children. And that is exactly where Paul goes next, in the first two verses of chapter 5: children imitating their parents.

People sometimes wonder which of our parents we most re-semble. Does she have her mother's chin? Does he have his father's walk? Our older daughters now sound like Emily when we hear them on the phone. They use some of the same expressions and have the same tone. The point of these opening verses in Ephesians 5 is not that we all have traits of nature and nurture that we take with us into marriage; the point is that there are traits that ought to characterize the family of God. And these family traits are seen preeminently in our elder brother Jesus Christ in both his love and his self-sacrifice.

If we are to imitate Christ in our marriage, we will love others by sacrificing. That does not mean that we will always do what our parents or our children most want. Even Christian parents and children have wants that must be delayed or denied. It does not even mean that we will always know what to say. What we do know is that challenges in family relations are contexts in which we can proactively extend the love of Christ to others, perhaps showing the gospel even if we can't solve a problem. What it does mean is that by God's grace we will do all that it takes to help make leaving and cleaving (or whatever the challenge might be) more manageable for our parents, and honoring and obeying easier for our children.

8

Bedtime in Marriage

RECOMMENDED READING

I CORINTHIANS 7:1–5

If a marriage was a house, intimate relations would be the closet, the place you don't show others, and which can be neglected to the point of becoming a mess. Where this happens, it is always a problem because physical intimacy, often leading to sexual intimacy, is part of the marriage package; in fact, it has been so from the beginning. Our first parents were supposed to see one another's nakedness (Gen. 2:25), to "become one flesh" (Gen. 2:24), and to be fruitful and multiply (Gen. 1:28).

Even the fall of humanity into sin has not changed this design and purpose for marriage. That said, like every aspect of life in a subnormal world, sin makes marital intimacy more difficult. Or to put it the other way, marriage offers yet another context for sinful abuse of a good thing. God told Adam that he would do his day's work in the midst of weeds and rocks. Time has shown that evenings for married couples together can become thorny, hard places too. Some marriages begin with sad sexual histories of abuse, rebellion, or disease. Marital intimacy can also be complicated by relational complexities such as remarriage after death or divorce. All of these topics deserve careful consideration, but the purpose of this chapter (designed especially for the married or almost married) is to offer a positive way forward. We want to reflect on God's words about God's gift of sexual intimacy to married couples.

What Is Intimacy For?

Early in the book we asked what marriage is for. In this chapter we ask what sexual intimacy is for. As we see it, the Scriptures tell us that marital intimacy has at least four purposes, and therefore sex can be used in marriage for any or all of them. (1) Sex is a bond in marriage, a way of expressing and reinforcing the marital union. (2) It is a proven way of filling the world with babies. (3) It is intended for our pleasure. And (4), as the apostle Paul sees it, it is a way in which we serve our spouse.

A Bond in Marriage

It is quite possible to be happy and fulfilled in life without sexual intercourse. Many single people testify to this today, as singles have done for centuries. At the same time, we can also say that from the beginning, the two were made to become one. Human oneness or unity is expressed in a variety of ways—by the way in which we seek agreement, share a purpose, or worship one Lord. But those bonds are merely intensifications of common or Christian forms of unity. The bond of marriage offers another variety of intimacy. We can see this in 1 Corinthians 7.

In the opening verses of 1 Corinthians 7 the apostle Paul offers an extended discussion of sexual relations. He is answering a question about whether it is good to avoid sex. His answer is multifaceted, but one part of that answer is that it is not good to avoid or withhold sex in marriage.

Paul's comments indicate the importance of our physicality. His words also remind us of the presence of temptation. Paul assumes that sexual activity is for married persons only. He says at the beginning and the end of the paragraph that sexual activity in marriage is designed in part to keep the marriage union together— to avoid the temptation of sharing ourselves with someone else (1 Cor. 7:2, 5). Paul's teaching presumes, in turn, that not only our hearts but also our bodies belong to the other. That is why the wife has a right to her husband's sexual attentions, and he to hers (7:3).

Paul goes so far as to say that a wife and a husband have a kind of control over each other's bodies and that to refuse sexual intercourse is to "deprive" one's spouse (7:5).[13] Contrary to almost all cultural norms, Christians insist both that men and women have conjugal rights and that a spouse does not have authority over his or her own body, while the partner does.[14] These are radical ideas, not only in Paul's day but in our own. Much can be learned about a Christian theology of the bedroom from the concept of *conjugal rights* coupled with the idea of *mutual authority* over the body of a spouse.

To say something negatively, as Paul does in verse 5, conjugal rights require that any suspension of "together time" as a couple must be discussed together, must be temporary, and must be for important reasons. Of course *no* might simply mean "later" while someone takes a few hours of sleep to recharge batteries. But if sexual intercourse is to be put on ice, it needs a unanimous vote. If this is true, it is likely the case that couples should also talk through other reasons for seasons of abstinence, such as recovery from birth or travel for work. Chad has found that he has to limit the frequency and duration of his trips from home in order to avoid temptation; as much as possible, we decide together how often and how long he should be gone. Where there is no interest in sexual relations on the part of one or both partners, we need to see this as an urgent problem to address together through pastoral care, counseling, or perhaps very wise friends.

To say something positively, because sexual relations strengthen a bond, married couples should regularly "come together" sexually. Whether that is four times a week or four times a month (stipulating a frequency would be unwise, to say the least), sexual intercourse needs to be the norm and not the exception in marriage, even while Christians recognize that different seasons in life call for different frequencies. The main point is that marital intimacy is intended to maintain and strengthen the bond of marriage. Only in unusual circumstances, such as a spouse with chronic sickness, could one hope for God's blessing on a marriage without sexual intercourse.

Babies in Marriage

Sexual intimacy is intended to strengthen the bond of marriage. But as one of the prophets put it, through Christian marriage God also seeks "godly offspring" (Mal. 2:15). Sexual intercourse is the usual course for getting that process started, and married Christian couples'must play their part in filling the earth (Gen. 1:28). That said, two qualifiers are in order.

First, there are marriages that face extraordinary health problems that make procreation challenging or dangerous. In such cases (and in other contexts) adoption is a wonderful gift to parents and children alike.

Second, sexual intimacy is intended for more than one purpose. For that reason we think that forms of birth control can be legitimate, provided that we are open to the Lord giving us children at some plausible point in our marriage, even if that requires shortening or changing a career in order to have one or more children. We also think that the Lord is seeking a godly seed or offspring from his people rather than just any kind of seed. This may have bearing on the question of birth control also; arguably, only a subset of parents are able to raise large families that are also godly families.

This topic offers a slippery path on which to walk. There are people who wish to have a small family because they don't want to be inconvenienced or to be challenged in their life; we must study our hearts in this matter, for we are called to lean on the Lord in all things, including family building. Nonetheless, in our judgment, nonabortive birth control is a plausible stewarding of our limited personal bandwidth and parenting resources as well as other gifts we have been given and are called to use.[15]

Bodies in Marriage

A third purpose for sexual intercourse is to foster marital intimacy through physical pleasure. God designed us and cares for us as embodied creatures, and he has also designed sexual intercourse to help us love one another better, with all that we are and all that we have. It is clear, for example, that in the context of marriage, our reproductive organs are intended to multitask. In fact, various parts of our bodies designed for nonreproductive reasons are still celebrated in Scripture for their sexual attractiveness.

With tasteful metaphor, chapters 4 and 5 of the Song of Solomon unmistakably celebrate the deliciousness of lovers' bodies and not merely their utility for making babies. Wise people have noted that this appears to be a theme in the Wisdom Literature. At least five places in three chapters celebrate the woman's breasts without any metaphor at all (Song 4:5; 7:3, 7, 8; 8:10). The book of Proverbs commands men to ravish themselves with their wife's breasts: "Let her breasts fill you at all times with delight; be intoxicated always in her love" (5:19). Our point is that a woman's breasts are designed to give milk, and yet this part of the human anatomy, involved in human nurture but not in the act of procreation, is commended here and in the Song of Solomon and elsewhere for sexual attention, as are lips, the neck, and other parts of the body.

The marriage bed is to be kept pure (Heb. 13:4). But it is hard to resist the conclusion that purity within marriage allows for our whole bodies to be used for sexual intimacy.

Submitting to One Another

Sexual intimacy expresses the bond of marriage, enables us to bring children into God's world, and gives us a way to delight in the body of a spouse. But when considering sex in marriage, the overall point of 1 Corinthians 7 is especially important for us to understand, for in the concepts of conjugal rights and mutual authority, we are once more hearing an echo of the dynamic revealed in Ephesians 5.

Unless you skipped right to this chapter, you will remember from earlier chapters that in submitting to one another, a husband or a wife is not to consider the other's duty in order to *direct* them, but to graciously *help* make their duty as pleasant as possible. This applies to marital intimacy also.

If a wife is supposed to give herself over to her husband sexually, then he should try to make that as pleasant as he can for her. She will find it hard to love him in bed if he has been unkind in the kitchen (after all, most problems in the bedroom don't start in the bedroom and aren't fixed in the bedroom). And for him to make her duty easier, he should try to be helpful and gentle all day long. As well, he should shower, maybe shave, and certainly make efforts to keep himself fit—not forever young, but fit for his age. He should care for his health not simply for himself or his family but to make himself attractive to his wife.

He should seek to wear (or not wear) and do (or not do) what pleases her. Here too he should study his wife. He should heed her communications, both spoken and unspoken. He should generally take his time in making love: as *slow* as possible, rather than the often selfish ASAP (as *soon* as possible), which starts with a glance at his wife, moves to a hasty conclusion, and ends with him snoring, all within a record-setting three minutes.

This runs the other way too. If he is supposed to give himself to her sexually, then she should make that as pleasant as possible for him. She should try to make herself look and smell presentable. Since many men are visually stimulated, attractive pieces of clothing will usually go a long way. Some kinds of evening wear are cozy but do not fire the imagination. They have their place, but we need to recognize that they can serve as armor against amour.

What is more, if he is to give himself to her, then she should not only acquiesce to sex; she should ask for it in some way or other (words are very effective here). Consent for sexual intercourse is important, but mere consent is uninspiring. Regular requests for sex are one of the most powerful ways of improving marital intimacy and the marriage itself. This sometimes, but not always, takes more work for women than men; people are wired differently, and their appetites for sex can differ too.

In saying all this, we are not interested in taking mystery out of intimacy. But it may help if a wife indicates what pleases her and what doesn't, if she knows. Early in a marriage, or on any given day in a marriage, she might not, and her husband can offer her some ideas without insisting on them. And needless to say, it will help a marriage if husband and wife continue to privilege the importance of intimate relations even after the arrival of children.

A word about *authority*. If we have authority over our spouse's body, it means that we can ask for a lot from the person we love! But we are saved sinners, not perfected saints, so this will always be a work in progress. Most of us will on occasion need to talk about what pleases us. This can be overdone. But most of the time it is underdone, especially at the beginning of marriage, and when our bodies begin to slow down. Don't just think it. Ask it. Our spouse may accept our requests more often than we expect, even when he or she is tired or feeling subpar.

Remember too that another's authority over our body is limited to marriage but not to the bedroom. It may find expression on a bed or off the bed, in the shower or in the car. Let your imagination be your friend. Sometimes there is good reason to put an interested spouse on hold when he or she is wanting the right thing at the "wrong" time or place; sometimes there is not.

On the other hand, because we want to make the exercise of our authority as easy as possible for our spouse to handle, a husband should not demand of his wife, or she of him, what the other finds demeaning or dangerous or exhausting or painful. To do so would not be kind and loving; it would seek to dominate the other rather than submit to the other; it would be to do the opposite of what Scripture says to do, which can never end well. But these desires should be discussed, for it may be that a good thing has been tarnished by our culture's crudeness, or that a somewhat uncomfortable thing can become pleasurable with proper help.

It remains to say something about timing, for so much literature on marriage and sex, some of it intended to avoid selfishness, stresses the importance of simultaneous orgasm and all the techniques to get there. This could be a good thing for a marriage. But we should note that Scripture directs our focus to the other person—how to please him or her, how to make as enjoyable as possible a mutual submission in the bedroom. As it happens, that kind of other mindedness often ends up in a very good place, it can itself be a sufficient goal for marital intimacy. As we see it, only if both partners concur should a shared climax be elevated to an important objective. But even then we think it is at least worth saying that some goals can be intimacy stoppers rather than intimacy starters. A less programmed search for pleasure can often make sex more pleasurable—and sometimes yield the same results.

Bring It into the Bedroom

As you can tell, we are counseling couples to take their Bible knowledge with them into the bedroom. That is not to say that quoting Bible verses, at least outside of the Song of Solomon, is a good idea for increasing intimacy. In fact, many things are intimacy killers, and if we are going to love one another thoughtfully, we should avoid saying, "Do you think the guests enjoyed dinner tonight?" and, "Did you feed the dog?" just as things are heating up. We have topics that we don't discuss after eight o'clock at night. If they come up, nothing else will.

More than avoiding intimacy killers, we need to cultivate intimacy builders. Again, this begins not five minutes before bed but in the way in which we treat each other all day, the way we look at each other, help each other, affirm each other, touch each other, talk to, and even flirt with each other.

In spite of all our best efforts, this does not always work. Titus 3:3 talks about how we used to be "slaves to various passions and pleasures." Sometimes we still struggle with old masters, or old memories, and this struggle can impact us in bed. As best as we can, we must try to focus on the one whom God has given to us and not allow the accuser to remind us of what happened before marriage. We can neither permit our minds to dwell on what happened in a previous relationship nor paint with our imagination what might be possible in a new relationship.

We can help one another with this. Yes, if our spouse is sinning in his or her mind, or in some other way, the sin is not ours. But it should be our hope to help our spouse avoid temptation and distraction through our own passion. Unfulfilled spouses are most likely to indulge in fantasy, self-pleasuring, and pornography, all of which express unfaithfulness. The best defense is a good offense. So let us pursue sexual relations actively, not passively.

Paradoxically, this will need to get more creative and persistent as libido lags; it is even more important for us to pursue one another actively where desire is retained but sexual machinery does not respond as readily as before. In marriage all is exposed.

It may be embarrassing, but if we love one another, we will talk about and find solutions to these problems that go beyond the measures recommended in sitcoms or commercials.

Hope in the Midst of Struggles

Sometimes everything goes right. When that happens, let us not forget the one who gave us to each other. Do you like your spouse's body? Thank God that he has given us a sense of beauty and proportion. Did you enjoy your spouse? Thank God that he gave us bodies.

Sometimes we will fail in the bedroom. We don't mean that we will not have as good a time as we planned. That happens. Sometimes sex is a simple snack and at other times a gourmet meal. That's okay. When we speak of failure, we mean that sometimes we say what we should not; we privilege ourselves over the other; we deprive the other in order to make a point or because we are indifferent or uncaring or insensitive. Here, especially, we need to think theologically, not least because our world supplies us with all kinds of hokey advice.

It is at times like this that we must thank God for who he is and what he does. Were you interrupted? God is sovereign over the events that led to your frustration. Do you not understand your spouse? God can give you wisdom. Did she just want to sleep after an eighteen-hour day? God is generous toward us in our weakness; let us pass that on. Did he speak sharply? Work it out—but then don't hold out. God is a God of forgiveness.

Consider the fruit of the Spirit: what could it mean for marital intimacy to be gentle or self-controlled (Gal 5:23)? Consider Paul's ode to love: what could the marriage bed look like if you kept no record of wrongs (1 Cor. 13:5)? Bringing theology into the bedroom doesn't mean that we need to get weird and declare sex sacred or sacramental. We simply need to remember who God is and who he calls us to be.

Sometimes we encounter a complete lack or breakdown of marital intimacy. Sickness, abuse, divorce, death, or maybe a dream of marriage that never materialized in the first place. Something keeps us from experiencing what we hoped for in this life. If you have ever been in the place of sexual disappointment or despair, and perhaps no one knows it but God, remember that Jesus came to fulfill all righteousness and that he was tempted in every way that we are, yet without sin. This means at least two things.

First, if Jesus is your Savior, then the sexual purity of Jesus is credited to your account as if it were yours, and the same is true for your spouse.

Second, whatever is meant by the marriage supper of the Lamb, it promises a union that is not sexual but is nonetheless true. There will be no regrets in heaven, no "if onlys" when we meet our Savior face to face.

Our hope is that sexual intimacy will not be the neglected closet of your marriage. The God of the day is also the God of your evenings, and his word is sufficient for this aspect of your marriage too. So may he use your intimate relations as a way of expressing and deepening your union with each other, granting you godly children, and bringing you a pleasure that will please the Father who made you and takes care of you.

9

Growing in Marriage

RECOMMENDED READING

I CORINTHIANS 7:32–35; I PETER 4:9

No study of marriage is complete without considering how we can grow in usefulness not only in the context of marriage and family but also in the context of our community, especially the household of God.

Between these covers we have offered a biblical definition of marriage, a history of marriage, and a perspective on marriage that emphasizes our opportunity to help our spouse in his or her calling before the Lord. We wanted to end by thinking about how we can help our spouse grow in the context of marriage. Here we could go almost anywhere. We decided to focus on what seems to us to be three key topics: (1) growing in usefulness, (2) growing in grace, and (3) growing in years.

Growing in Usefulness

Married people often spot ways in which they can be a blessing to those around them. They can coach a team, contribute to a neighborhood association, or support a political organization.

They can reach out together, like Priscilla and Aquila, to teach new Christians how to read the Bible (Acts 18:26). They can together contribute to the needs of the saints (Rom. 12:13). They can open their homes to host a group or house church, like Philemon, and perhaps Apphia (Philem. 1:1–2). They might help younger couples in the faith who are approaching marriage. Just as we don't want to be self-focused as individuals, we don't want to be self-focused as couples. Just as we want to help our spouse with his or her calling as a spouse, so too we want to help our spouse live out Christian duties more generally.

One example of the way in which spouses can help one another to serve is in showing hospitality. Married couples can make their home a haven especially for people who are traveling, new to the area, or in need of some Christian family time. Paul calls everyone to hospitality (Rom. 12:13). Peter tells us in one of his letters to think about our attitude toward hospitality (1 Pet. 4:9). The epistle to the Hebrews highlights the importance of using hospitality to care for strangers (Heb. 13:2). In today's mobile global culture there are more travelers, more people passing through, and perhaps more loneliness than ever before. Experts argue that the extent to which loneliness afflicts our world appears to be reaching almost pandemic proportions. So not only the Bible's encouragement but also our culture's needs lead us to flag hospitality as an example where couples might grow in usefulness together. If two can live more cheaply than one, they can also often host people more easily than one.

The example of hospitality is also useful as a case study of marital service because there are different gifts at play. There is the hard work of cleaning, the courage to invite, the ability to cook a meal, and the challenge of carrying on a conversation. Every part is necessary. If one is a good cook but too shy to invite someone over, gifts will not be used. But when we do help a spouse use gifts, then hosting someone on a Sunday might help the guest come to love the Lord's Day or become attached to a good church. We make our guest's Christian life richer and bring praise to God.

As it happens, this is a real-life example. Emily finds it easier to cook for twenty than to extend an offer to cook for two. Chad can invite people over but his weakness, of almost legendary proportions, is that when he cooks, no one is ever hungry enough to eat what he makes. Prior to marriage, innocents would still arrive for Sunday lunch, but as word got out, counterproposals became the norm. Most people would invite him to their home or volunteer to cook. Friends thought it was a bachelor trick.

The real point here is that while many singles manage to be Mary and Martha at the same time (Luke 10.38–42), married couples sometimes have an advantage in engaging in conversation and meal preparation at a competent level. In our home, Chad leads the tidying team and greets guests at the door; Emily feeds them.

For service to work, we need to remind our spouse that this is not all about ourselves. In other words, hospitality is not entertainment. Today, entertainment suggests that great food and good dishes be used and that the hosts be fresh and attentive, the house presentable for guests. Entertainment can be wonderful. But it is usually done for the pleasure of the hosts as much as for the guests. It is not to be confused with service per se.

Hospitality is very different. It is sometimes exercised when entertainment would not be. Hospitality can involve serving leftovers or hot dogs. It might involve bringing people into a house that has not been readied. Perhaps a caveat can be issued to explain that nothing fancy will be served. But the point is that hospitality is extended to facilitate fellowship, not because it is convenient for ourselves (although we usually enjoy our guests)!

The apostle Peter calls us to show hospitality without grumbling (1 Pet. 4:9). Truth be told, we sometimes set up spouses for grumbling by not thinking ahead or by surprising our spouse with visitors. Couples can make these moments more manageable by stocking up with some easy meals in the freezer, by encouraging each other to remember that service is for others, by not making hospitality just one more job on top of the others that a main cook or cleaner of the house must absorb, or by planning ahead.

We've said that married couples sometimes have an advantage in hospitality, and there are other advantages beside those we've mentioned. For instance, a married couple can invite over a single man or a married woman in contexts that may be inappropriate for a single man or woman. Hospitality offers one example of how couples can grow in usefulness together.

As we consider growing in usefulness, we recall that the apostle Paul focuses in 1 Corinthians 7:32–35 on ways in which singles can uniquely use their gifts. Especially in the context of service, singleness is a worthy calling, and in some contexts a preferred calling. Among the benefits of the single life is the lack of anxiety about the needs and wants of a spouse. As much as we might be working together to serve others, husbands and wives are often (legitimately) focused on pleasing and serving the other. The apostle Paul highlights the ways in which the unmarried can offer undivided devotion to the Lord. Indeed, some of the most useful Christians in the past century have been single people, living for the benefit of others and the pleasure of God. And some of the strongest Christians we know are single people, living life to the full, able to be flexible in the use of their gifts, including their time and money. Many of these singles have helped us exercise hospitality as a family by playing games with our younger children or helping us set the table, prepare food, or clean up. One single friend would sometimes show up unannounced after hearing that we had hosted people for a meal and do the dishes for us while we were putting children to bed.

But we are writing a book on marriage, and our point here is simply that married couples must consider ways in which they can leverage their marriage through opportunities specially suited for twosomes (even if assisted by others), and by considering how we make it easier for our spouse to use gifts in service to Christ.

Growing in Grace

This focus about usefulness *in* marriage is sometimes useful *for* marriage. When a marriage is weak or struggling, couples can sometimes help each other, not by focusing more on their own marriage but by focusing on others.

In the early years of our marriage, Chad ran the risk of analyzing our relationship to death. Too many sit-down-and-think-it-all-through discussions. Too many state-of-the-union addresses. Over time it occurred to us that a shared purpose in serving others would not only honor Christ but would also prove to be one of the best ways of giving us greater harmony in our marriage.

Growing in usefulness helps us to grow in grace and grow together. We are not saying that busyness can replace thoughtfulness. We are saying that without a shared purpose in serving as a married couple, a relationship can turn inward in unhelpful ways, and serving together helps to avoid that problem in a way that always entertaining ourselves, or often talking about ourselves, does not. Mind you, the main purpose of serving others *is* serving others. The benefit to ourselves is a bonus, a probable side effect leading to a boost for our marriage.

The best way for married people to grow is by making full use of the means of grace, such as prayer and the sacraments and the word of God. These gifts from God are designed to help all people—including married people—learn wisdom, live out their identity in Christ, and find the freedom of forgiveness. This is important to mention because married life can magnify foolishness, shame, and sin.

Foolishness

It is easy in a marriage to drift into foolish patterns. When we see faults in others, or even in ourselves, we sometimes try to escape or build walls to create safe spaces where no one else can harm us. At other times we go on the attack, cultivating snappy one-liners that will put the other down or at least in their place. It appears to cost us nothing to stockpile grievances or criticisms to fire at our "enemy." Yet none of this is helpful. All of it calls for wisdom.

If we are humbled before God, we can move beyond how we'd like to act and consider how we ought to act. If we live *coram Deo*, before the face of God, we will relate to others first by relating to him. In any conflict, the fear of God is the beginning of wisdom (Prov. 9:10). We want this for our spouses, so let us pray for their growth in wisdom and not try to change them by ourselves. Let's give them time to read, think, pray (and pray some more), and space to reflect rather than offering in-your-face correction as a help for their sanctification.

Shame

Marriage can also magnify shame. No one in this world comes to know us better than a spouse. This knowledge has the potential for great good. And yet in this closest of friendships, people also see our worst faults and not simply our greatest strengths. We often care about our spouse's opinion more than anyone else's. That is a position of power, and we can encourage each other more than anyone else. But when we fail a spouse, or fail in front of a spouse, or think we have done so, our marital relationship has both the capacity to convey more hope and kindness or to bottle up and hold more shame than any other social unit. For that reason, we must use our influence with our spouse with care, remembering that we are accountable for how we treat one another.

Now *his* real dignity and identity should not be found in *her* opinion. When he cares too much about her words or thoughts, he will not confess sin in front of her, or he will despair, or he will devalue their relationship so that her disapproval will matter less. And likewise for wives.

We need to remember the one who was humbled for our sakes, who bore the shame of our sin and failings, so that we could be identified with him in this life both in his humiliation and in his exaltation. The best way to help our spouse find a Christ-centered glory in the midst of our shame is for us to trust in him ourselves and value our identity in Christ above all. That means thanking him for our successes instead of boasting, and trusting him with our failures instead of despairing. Good examples even between spouses are powerful blessings.

It might also involve thinking with our spouse about the sacraments or ordinances of baptism and the Lord's Supper. In baptism God puts his own triune name on us. What dignity this gives to those who struggle with self-loathing to know that they are loved by the Lord! In the Lord's Supper we fellowship by faith, in weakness, with the Father, through the Son, by the power of the Holy Spirit. What a privilege to have close communion with such a God.

Sin

Christian marriage is, in the third place, a context in which we learn more about sin. For any change to happen in a marriage, and in the people in the marriage, we need an awareness of sin. The long-term, close proximity of one person with the other does this wonderfully. First we see the sin of others. Then we see our own. First we see what inconveniences and irritates us. Then we come to an honest awareness of who we are before our spouse and before God. It is only when we look at God that we learn how to see ourselves rightly.

It is when husbands and wives see themselves as sinners trusting in Christ, when we see ourselves as the rich beneficiaries of the grace of God, that we learn to dole out mercy to others too. This is how we learn about forgiveness. This is how we love like saints. If we have a Godward focus, we will take 100 percent of the responsibility for our contribution to any conflict, no matter what the percentage of our part of the problem might be. We'll confess that before God and before our spouse or whomever we have offended. We'll do that because the sting and penalty of our sin are taken away.

This is how a Christian spouse can thrive even in the midst of a marriage that has not thrived. It is not by perpetually blaming or fighting or even by changing; it is by seeing ourselves as God sees his children in Christ.

Chad remembers speaking about this with a friend whose trust in a spouse had been steadily eroded over a period of years. The temptation for this friend to think that there must be a better way was very strong. And so they talked about that. This dear friend needed to trust the Lord.

As it turned out, our friend also needed to do some log removal (Matt. 7:3–5). Her spouse seemed so obviously at fault, and yet he thought the same thing about her, and this friend had no credibility until she was willing to confess her own sin. Only then could their war of words begin to be addressed. And that, in turn, made space for real conversations, gentle restoration, and real reconciliation. There was a long way to go, but at least they had a new beginning.

The key in all of this is what Christ demonstrated to us: don't treat others as they deserve to be treated. Treat others as God has treated us, including in marriage. Yes, people are sinning against us. So we can now run them to the ground or cut them apart or bring justice on their heads, or we can remember that when we deserved punishment, God sent his Son to die on the cross in our place and for our good.

Yes, there are times when we cannot overlook a fault, and so we must try to work out a problem carefully and thoughtfully. But here too, we can work it out like those prosecuting attorneys who advertise on billboards, taking a cut of any case they win. Or, as one prominent Christian ministry emphasizes, we can try to work things out with the goal of blessing another person and restoring a relationship.

God's mercy must inform our marriages because the gospel contains a logic for relationships. If God truly promises to forgive a husband in Christ Jesus, that man must truly promise to forgive his wife. If God does not dwell on her foolishness, she should not dwell on her husband's. If God does not bring up incidents again in order to shame us, nor should we. If God covers over our sins, we should cover over the sins of our spouse. If God will never let sin against him stand between him and his children, we cannot allow incidents to stand as walls in a marriage. And when we show this kind of grace toward our spouse, it makes it easier for our spouse to show it back.

How do we come to think this way? How do we remember these truths? By reading the word, by hearing the preaching of the word, and by thinking and talking about what we've read and heard with Christian friends, including our spouse.

Growing in Years

Christian couples long to grow in grace together. But there is one more kind of growing that we hope to do with each other as married people: growing old. Not many people actually want to be old. But we want to be together, even when we're old.

Growing old is not for the faint of heart. Bodies hurt. Things stop working. A point comes in every person's life when we top out and begin to decline. We are more tired after doing less, we recognize more people in the obituary column, and often our memories begin to fade. Long before all that happens, there comes a day when most of us realize that some of our dreams will never be fulfilled. These moments appear amid seasons of transition in which we must help each other reflect anew on who we are and what we are for.

One thing we can help each other do is to stop idealizing what we were when we were younger. Emily's father performed this service through a wry comment to Chad: "When you are older and forgetful, you'll think it's because of your age. When that happens, try to remember that you were always forgetful!"

Growing in years ought to offer one consolation for a Christian: if we are joined to Jesus by faith, his strength will be on display in our weakness. Here especially, older Christian couples can encourage each other. We can remind each other of how, in our lifetime, we learned to see the gospel not simply as information but as power. We can recall our spiritual poverty and how we learned, as the years went by, how rich we are in Jesus Christ. God has been generous beyond all imagining! He has united us to his own Son; he has freely justified us before the throne of God above; he has graciously adopted us into his family; he has begun his sanctifying work in us by his Holy Spirit.

One reason why we are to respect the elderly is that some element of growing in grace usually only happens as we grow in years. And it is this growth in grace, and not simply a growth in love for one another, that makes many white-haired marriages so wonderful. They've learned that with their sins forgiven, they can repent and ask forgiveness with a new thoroughness. Knowing that they are clothed in the righteousness of Jesus Christ, they no longer need to hide behind their own imagined holiness. They no

longer need to escape those who point out their wrongs by denying or fleeing, by attacking or overcoming their critics, because
they are secure in Christ their Savior.

Conclusion

It is our prayer that the saved sinners who read this book on marriage will grow to love like the saints that Christ has redeemed us
to be. For as our gracious God answers our prayers, we will find
in his church the kinds of marriages that mirror the gospel and
offer a foretaste of heaven even in this fallen world. Husbands and
wives who seek their spouse's joy will find joy in their callings.
They will be increasingly content both in easy times and hard,
with family and in private. And all the while they will be growing
in usefulness, and growing in grace, as they grow in years—and
all to the glory of God.

Appendix

How to Change Your Spouse
in Three Easy Steps

THIS APPENDIX CONTAINS everything we know about changing your spouse.

Discussion Questions

Chapter 1: The Bible and Marriage

1. What would you like to get out of a study on marriage?

2. Do you have insights on marriage? How would you capture them in a chapter title or two?

3. How might learning about marriage—the challenges, temptations, responsibilities, and blessings—be useful to a single person?

4. Are you eager to conform your marriage, or your idea of a good marriage, to God's revealed will for marriage as presented in the Bible? Why or why not?

5. What do you think of this definition of marriage: "Marriage is a God-given, lifelong, publicly recognized, exclusive bond between a man and a woman"? Why is each part of this description important? Does anything need to be added or removed?

6. How does Matthew 6:33—"Seek first the kingdom of God and his righteousness, and all these things will be added to you"— guide us in our engagements and marriages?

7. What are five purposes for marriage? How are they supported biblically? Do you see each one as important? Do you need to appreciate one of these purposes more than you have in the past?

Chapter 2: History and Marriage

1. How would you describe the four stages of redemptive history and what do they tell you about marriage?

2. How can keeping the big picture in mind help you in your marriage? How can it give you hope? How can it redirect your focus when needed?

3. How might you have treated your marriage like an idol? How might you have treated your spouse like one?

4. How often are your problems in marriage exacerbated because you act like you're in Eden, expecting more from a spouse, or from your marriage, than your place in redemptive history allows? Can you think of a specific example?

5. Marriage can improve after the fall and before Christ's return. What might that look like? What should be our expectations of a good marriage?

Chapter 3: Grace in Marriage

1. What associations does submission have for you? To what extent does the definition "respecting that leads to serving" reflect the biblical meaning? How could this definition help you in your marriage?

2. For couples, have you had your own EMOJI experience in your marriage? What is God showing you about your spouse's specific likes and dislikes? How could you study your spouse more?

3. Consider your spouse's duties as described in Ephesians 5. How might a marriage change if a spouse tried to make it easier for the other to fulfill his or her duties?

4. Wives, are there ways you make it easier for your husband to love you? To provide for you? Husbands, are there ways you make it easier for your wife to respect you?

5. How is God encouraging you to be a gracious spouse? Is God showing you ways that you postpone serving your spouse until you yourself are served first? How does the pattern of God's love both convict and encourage you?

6. How can the way you treat your spouse show reverence for Christ? What passage of Scripture encourages this Christian grace? What power does the Holy Spirit offer us in marriage? Where can you specifically draw upon the Holy Spirit's help?

7. In light of this study, how would you like to pray for your marriage or the marriage of someone you know?

Chapter 4: Women and Marriage

For wives:

1. What does submission look like in your marriage? What words would you use to describe it?

2. How can you cultivate a positive image of Christian submission? What negative portrayals do you need to correct or oppose?

3. How do you know when you have crossed the line from presenting options in a marriage to demanding?

4. Can you let your husband make poor decisions and trust God to work them for good? What might this look like?

5. Can you recall a time when your husband spared you from making a bad decision? A time when, if he had followed your advice, you actually would have been disappointed later on?

6. Are there people in your life who set positive examples of submission? Would it be helpful to ask them how they work through challenges in this aspect of their lives?

For husbands:

1. In light of your wife's duties, how can you support her in prayer?

2. Where might it be helpful to refrain from calling for a wife to submit?

3. Where might you delegate more decisions to your wife?

4. Can you better encourage her in the decisions that she makes? How?

Chapter 5: Men and Marriage

For husbands:

1. What are the models for marital love that the apostle Paul commends to husbands?

2. What motives or reasons for love does Scripture present?

3. How does Ephesians 5 help you think about and deal with persistent sin in your wife or in you?

4. What would it look like for you to take new steps in loving your wife with all that you are and all that you have? What changes would need to be made in your life if you were to be like Christ by loving your wife deeply, sacrificially, faithfully, purposefully?

5. Are you praying for your wife and studying her so that you can pray for her better? If so, what have you learned? How have your prayers for her developed over time?

6. What are your aims in your prayers? Is the prayer really for her? Or for you? What answers can be seen to your prayers?

7. Are you leading devotions that profit your wife? How might you shape your study of the Bible and Christian doctrine so that what you say will be thoughtful and useful to her?

8. As you lead your wife, how can you communicate that you love her and avoid the problem of making every moment with you feel like it was a teaching moment for her?

9. Do you give her time to study God's word herself, or with friends? Are there any changes that could be made on your part that would benefit her in her walk with the Lord?

For wives:

1. In light of your husband's duty to love you, how might you pray for him? Has God answered this kind of prayer before for you? If so, how?

2. Are you willing to entrust to God your husband's ability to love you? What does that trust look like?

3. As lovable as you already are to your husband, what might you do to make it even easier for your husband to love you? Similarly, how can you encourage your husband in loving you well?

4. Love takes many forms. How might you recognize your husband's current actions as an expression of his love for you?

5. How can you support your husband's spiritual growth so that, in turn, he can better lead you spiritually?

Chapter 6: Winning in Marriage

1. How would you put the "winning" strategy in 1 Peter 2 into your own words? What is the hope in it?

2. For wives, how might the Lord use your inner beauty to win over your husband, either to initial faith in Christ or greater growth in grace?

3. For wives, are there fears that you must overcome in prioritizing inner beauty? If so, what are they? How does God's word speak to these fears?

4. For husbands, given your wife's weakness, are there ways you are tempted to sin against her? If so, where do you need to repent, and what grace do you need to grow in?

5. Learning about the other gender is complicated and takes honest work. What has God taught you about your spouse recently? How do you plan to learn more?

6. In light of 1 Peter 3:7, what reasons does God give for why a husband should honor his wife? Considering your marriage in particular, how would you like to honor your wife?

7. Many messages of grace are offered that one spouse can send to the other: tell spouses that they are coheirs of grace; you are no better; you love them in their failings; and others. What message of grace do you want to give to your spouse today?

8. What would you like someone to learn about the gospel through your role as a spouse, even in difficult situations?

9. How does 1 Peter 3 direct you to pray for one another?

Chapter 7: Family and Marriage

1. Consider how you can make the "leaving and cleaving" process easier for others:

   - If you are married, how can you make it easier for parents to let you leave? What will your adjusted contact with them look like? How can you assure them of your ongoing love for them, even while prioritizing your marriage?

   - Are there ways that you are still cleaving to your parents? When facing a problem, is your first impulse to talk to your parents or your spouse? When given exciting news, whom do you want to tell first?

   - If you are a parent of a married child, how can you make it easier for your adult child to prioritize the marriage relationship? Can you take the children for a weekend? Babysit?

Perhaps hire a babysitter for them, and not just when they are going on a date with you?

- For parents, are there ways that you expect your child to put your opinion before your son- or daughter-in-law's? How can you make it clear that you expect your opinion to count for less than your son- or daughter-in-law's?

- For parents, what example did your parents set for you in this transition? What do you want to copy? What do you want to do differently?

2. How can you make your spouse's job as a parent easier?

- For wives, how has God made you to help your husband be a godly father? What opportunities has God given you to support his position as head of the household in front of the children?

- For husbands, how has God made you to lead your wife as a godly mother? How can you make her duties more pleasant without doing her work for her? How can you help the children honor her authority in the home?

3. When you have an opinion differing from that of your spouse, how do you talk about it? How might God bless your marriage, and your children, if you didn't work out your differences in front of your children? What sacrifices would this require? Which diverging perspectives can be helpfully discussed before children?

4. For blended families, the "Gouge principle" (or Pauline principle!) of gracious relationships still applies.

    • What opportunities is God giving you to support your spouse as a stepparent? Where is God leading you to show compassion? Encouragement? Humility?

    • For stepparents, how can you help your stepchildren honor their biological parent?

    • How can you help your children honor your spouse as a stepparent?

5. For those who have had multiple marriages, how does the way you relate to an ex-spouse impact your present marriage? What can you do to communicate to your spouse that he or she is your number-one priority (after God)? Is there anything that God is showing you that you need to change in how you relate to your ex in order to give your present marriage its due place?

6. Consider how you can help one another to make the command to honor parents easier for your children. What opportunities is God giving you to make it easier for your children to honor you? Consider the following topics and how they can make it easier or harder for your kids to respect you. Jot down a few ideas.

    • how you speak to their friends and about them
    • your service at church and home
    • your work

- your dress
- your expression of emotions
- your prayers

Chapter 8: Bedtime in Marriage

1. Reflect on an attribute or a name of God. What implications does this have for your sexual relations? For example, God is true. Am I honest in my relations with my spouse? God is wise and good. Do I trust his commands for sexual relations in marriage, even when they aren't always the way I would choose on my own?

2. How is God leading you to grow in grace in your sexual life?

3. Choose a fruit of the Spirit. How could that be expressed in your sexual relations?

4. Is your sexual life a topic for regular prayer for you? How might God bless you if it were?

5. Consider the prayer acronym ACTS: adoration, confession, thanksgiving, supplication. Reflecting on your sexual life, what do you want to pray in each of these categories? In other words, what do you want to praise God for? What sins of omission and commission do you have to confess? Are there blessings in your sexual life for which you need to give thanks? Are there graces and blessings that you want to request?

Chapter 9: Growing in Marriage

1. How have other married couples served you in your life? If you are married, what opportunities is God giving you to serve others outside your marriage and family? How might this help you grow in Christ?

2. When your service to others falls short of what you would have liked, how do you cope? What are some facts about who God is and what he does that can help you persevere through these disappointments?

3. Are there times when you've served others as a couple and have had to depend on the Lord more? How did the Lord help you? How might he help you in a new area of service?

4. What stressful situations do you and your spouse typically face? When stress increases, do you act as allies or enemies? Knowing God is on your side, will you commit to being your spouse's ally? What might this look like?

5. The lesson notes that we can care about our spouse's opinion more than any other. Recognizing this sensitivity, how do you sometimes discourage your spouse? What opportunities is God giving you to encourage your spouse?

6. How does your spouse encourage you? Will you let him or her know? Is there a way you feel shamed or judged by your spouse? Can you imagine a useful way to discuss this? If your spouse

were to tell you ways that you have been discouraging, would you be ready to listen without being defensive? What might you remember about what God has done for you as you listen to this feedback from your spouse?

7. How might the Lord grow you if you focused first on removing the log from your own eye before the speck from your spouse's?

8. The lesson notes that sometimes when our spouse sins against us, we act like a prosecuting attorney who is ready to make a profit. What are signs that we are acting this way? How can we tell if we are seeking to bless the other person and restore a relationship?

9. As you look ahead to growing older in marriage, is it your goal to be able to ask forgiveness with thoroughness (even if it is not your spouse's goal)? What does that look like?

10. Are there ways that you avoid those who point out your wrongs? How does knowing God and what he has done for you help you freely face your mistakes and sins?

Notes

1. The civil magistrate, as given by God, may authorize and witness the marriage of a man and a woman.
2. John R. W. Stott, *The Message of Ephesians* (Leicester, UK: Inter-Varsity Press, 1979), 221.
3. Incidentally, because both husbands and wives thought he was giving away too much to the other spouse, Gouge offered a table of the "particular duties of wives" and set it over against the "particular duties of husbands," showing how each gift of generous service and love *from the one* corresponds to a gift of generous service and love *from the other*. He also offered a table of the particular sins of husbands and wives, explaining how we often use our privileged knowledge of someone else's duties to do them harm instead of doing them good.
4. This is a good thing, a wonderful blessing in a marriage, and one about which a wife should not feel guilty. Just as we engage all of our skills and wisdom in serving Christ in the rest of life, so too in marriage. Nonetheless, it is precisely because wives are to honor Christ by being preoccupied with their husbands that Paul reminds some women who want to honor Christ that they may prefer not to be married.
5. John Calvin, *Sermons on the Epistle to the Ephesians*, trans. A. Golding (1973; repr., Edinburgh: Banner of Truth, 1998), 123.
6. John Calvin, *Commentaries on the Epistle of Paul to the Galatians and Ephesians*, vol. 21, Calvin's Commentaries, trans. W. Pringle (Grand Rapids, MI: Baker, 1993), 317.
7. Stott, *Message of Ephesians*, 234.

8. John Chrysostom, *Homilies on Galatians, Ephesians, Philippians, Colossians, Thessalonians, Timothy, Titus, and Philemon*, Nicene and Post-Nicene Fathers, First Series; ed. Philip Schaff (Peabody, MA: Hendrickson, 1999), 144 (homily 20).

9. Peyton Reed, dir., *The Break-Up* (Los Angeles: Universal Pictures, 2006).

10. In recalling her history we're not sure if Peter is making a specific reference to Genesis 18 where, even in speaking to herself, she calls her husband her lord. If so, then Peter may mention it because it was an uncommon tribute to a husband in the ancient world, even where society was patriarchal. On the other hand, since Peter puts Sarah forward as a representative of how holy women adorn themselves, we think Peter is saying that this reflects the degree to which she respected her husband—a typical pattern of holy women of old, of whom Sarah (all faults considered) is exemplary.

11. For full disclosure, on rare occasions Emily talks about Chad's faults but chooses to do so with his godly mother, confident that she already understands the irritation and will encourage Emily in patience.

12. Hillary of Arles, "Introductory commentary on 1 Peter," in *Ancient Commentary on Scripture, New Testament XI: James, 1-2 Peter, 1-3 John, Jude*, ed. Gerald Bray (Downers Grove, IL: InterVarsity Press, 2000), 99–100.

13. Sadly, through much of Christian history and in many non-Christian cultures, only half of this truth is remembered, causing no end of suffering for women.

14. Conjugal rights are not the same as the Western world's concept of "sexual needs," for sex is not as necessary as food, shelter, and water, and many people do without it.

15. Some birth-control methods are not acceptable because rather than preventing conception they kill a baby.

General Index

abuse, 37–38, 59, 81, 100, 118
adoption, 111
age, matters in marriage, 19, 23
Apphia, 120
arranged marriage, 19
attentiveness in marriage, 40–42
Augustine, 26, 28, 29, 81, 95–96

baptism, 126
beauty, not external, 78–80
"be fruitful and multiply," 22
birth control, 111, 148n15
blended families, 100–101
Book of Common Prayer, 9
Break-Up, The (film), 77

Calvin, John, 50
childbirth, pain in, 83
child-centered marriage, 102
child-rearing, 101–3
children: as imitators of their parents, 104–5; nurtured in the faith, 22
Christian life, subverts cultural trends, 55
Christian marriage, illustrates the gospel, 72, 74

Christians: to marry other Christians, 19–21; as saints, 14; as sinners, 13
Chrysostom, John, 69
church growth, through marriage, 22
cohabitating couples, always on audition, 17
coheirs of the grace of life, 87–88, 89
common grace, 28
communication in marriage, 85–86
companionship in marriage, 22, 23
complacent deference, 58
confession of sin, 72–73
conjugal rights, 109, 112, 148n14
covenant, marriage as, 11
cultural norms in marriage, 17–18

desertion, 81
despair in marriage, 30
divorce, 118

Eden, marriage in, 26–27
Edwards, Jonathan, 96
Edwards, Sarah, 97
empty nest, struggles with, 103

entertainment vs. hospitality, 121
entrusting ourselves to God, 76
"evangelistic dating," 21
Eve, as Adam's helper, 61–62

faithfulness to Christ, 78
faithfulness in marriage, 90
fallen marriage, 27–29, 30
families, 9
fear of God, 124
fighting, 77–78
foolishness in marriage, 124–25
forgiveness, 31, 128
forgiveness in marriage, 104
Franklin, Benjamin, 15
fruit of the Spirit, 117

God: diplays strength in our weak-
    ness, 129; love for Israel, 66;
    redeems married people, 30
godly offspring, 111–12
gospel: contains logic for relation-
    ships, 128; illustrated in
    Christian marriage, 72, 74
Gouge, Elizabeth, 61
Gouge, William, 14, 39, 42, 43, 44,
    56, 147n3
growing in marriage, 119–30; in
    grace, 123–28; in usefulness,
    119–23; in years, 128–30

harshness, 72
head and body metaphor, 50, 51
headship in marriage, 44, 50–51
heavenly-mindedness in marriage,
    33
Henry, Matthew, 50
Hillary of Arles, 88
holiness, growth in, 65–68
honoring parents in marriage,
    98–100

hope in marriage, 30
hospitality, 120–22
husbands: created to love their
    wives, 70–71; different roles
    from wives, 52; honoring wives
    in their weakness, 82–84;
    to live with their wives in
    understanding way, 84–86; to
    love wives in Christlike way,
    64–65, 67; to love wives as
    they love themselves, 68, 73;
    to make submission easy, 52;
    respect for wives, 86–87

imitating Christ in our marriage,
    105
impatience, 72
improvement guide for spouses,
    43, 131
in-laws, 96–98
inner self-adornment of, 79–80
intimacy builders, 116
Israel, as unfaithful spouse, 66

Jesus Christ: and his body, 50; and
    the church, 70, 71; humbled
    for our sakes, 125; lordship
    in marriage, 11; love for his
    church, 63–64, 70; love and
    self-sacrifice of, 105; sexual
    purity of, 118; marriage with
    the church as his bride, 33–35;
    suffered as substitute and
    example, 76, 91

kindness and tenderness in mar-
    riage, 104
knowledge: of each other in mar-
    riage, 40–42; of Scripture,
    42–43

leadership, 70
leaving and cleaving, 94–95, 98, 103, 105
loneliness, 95, 120
longing for heaven, 95–96
Lord's Supper, 126
Luther, Martin, 54

marital intimacy, 107–18; and physical pleasure, 111–12; and procreation, 110–11; strengthens the bonds of marriage, 110
marriage: always ought to be consensual, 18; as civil ordinance, 17; comes before parenting, 102; in context of the gospel, 10; equips us for eternity, 33; in fourfold state, 26; as gift from God, 13, 16; growth in, 119 30; idolizing of, 33; as life-long commitment, 16, 18; as new alignment of affection and respect, 94; between one man and one woman, 15–16, 18; only context for sexual activity, 23; for personal fulfillment, 10; purpose of, 22; in redemptive history, 26–35; as a shadow, 35
marriage maximalism, 17
marriage supper of the lamb, 34–35, 118
means of grace, 67, 124
men and women, equality of, 52
Monica (mother of Augustine), 81
mutual authority, over body of a spouse, 109, 112–14
mutuality in marriage, 22, 87
mutual love and respect, 55, 73

mutual submission, 39, 44, 52, 55, 67; in the bedroom, 115
mystery of marriage, 71–73

one flesh, 68, 71, 94

parenting, as challenge to marriage, 101–104
Patricius (father of Augustine), 81
Paul: on love, 117–19; on sexual relations, 108–9; on submission, 38
perseverance in marriage, 31
persons and roles, 54
Philemon, 120
pilgrim marriages, 30–31
pornography, 116
prayers, unhindered in marriage, 89
praying together, 102
Priscilla and Aquila, 120
procreation, when challenging or dangerous, 110–11

race and nationality in marriage, 18, 23
reconciliation, 127
repentance to your spouse, 104
reproduction of the human race, through marriage, 22
reverence for Christ in marriage, 45–46
rich in Jesus Christ, 129
rights, 55. See also conjugal rights

sanctification, 65
Sarah, beauty of her character, 80
Scriptures, give husbands more instructions, 63
self-control, 70
sexual abstinence, seasons of, 110

sexual intimacy. See marital
    intimacy
shame in marriage, 125–26
sin, against your spouse, 104
singleness, 108, 122–23
sin in marriage, 126–28
Song of Solomon, 112
spiritual coldness, 90
state of glory, marriage in, 32–35
state of grace, marriage in, 29–32
state of innocence, marriage in,
    26–27
state of sin, marriage in, 27–29
stepparenting, 100
Stott, John, 51
submission, 37–38, 44; cultural
    challenges to, 54–55, 61; for
    everyone, 39–40; as an orien-
    tation in marriage, 56; part
    of the Christian life, 38; and
    relational dynamics, 60; rooted
    in creation not chauvinism,
    39; as service, 40; as a spiritual
    gift, 41; as too convenient,
    57–58; as too fuzzy, 56–57; as
    too hard, 59–61

suffering graciously, 82

temptation, 109; loveliness of, 80

unfaithfulness, corrosive to a mar-
    riage, 78
unhappiness in marriage, 33

weakness, 82–83
wedding supper of the Lamb. See
    marriage supper of the Lamb
wisdom, 124
withholding sex in marriage, 109
wives: different roles from hus-
    bands, 52; honor of, 88; not
    mere roommates, 85; to respect
    their husbands, 75; sanctifica-
    tion of, 65–68; submission to
    husbands, 47–62; submission
    not to men in general, 53; win-
    ning husbands without words,
    77–78
world, opposition to submission, 61

youth, idealizing of, 129

Scripture Index

Genesis
1 . . . . 15, 22
1:26–31 15
1:27 16
1:28 . . . . 107, 110
2 . . . . 16, 68, 94, 98
2:15–25 15
2:24 . . . . 11, 16, 107
2:25 107
3 25
3:15 29
3:16 60
12 80
18 . . . . 148n10
24:57–58 19

Exodus
20:12 98

Deuteronomy
5:16 98
6:10–7:5 20

Esther
1–2 20

Proverbs
5:19 112

9:10 124
19:11 98

Song of Solomon
4 112
4:5 112
5 112
7:3 112
7:7 112
7:8 112
8:10 112

Malachi
2:13–16 17
2:15 110

Matthew
1:18–25 29
6:33 134
7:3–5 127
22:30 32

Mark
10:9 16

Luke
3:23–38 29
10:38–42 121

Acts
18:26........120

Romans
8:7...........29
12:13........120

1 Corinthians
7.............20, 103, 108, 112
7:1–5.........107
7:2............23, 109
7:3............109
7:5............109
7:9............23
7:32–35......119, 122
7:36–38......19
7:39.........21
11:3.........50
11:11–12....50
13............26
13:5.........118
13:7.........27

2 Corinthians
1:3–4.........62
6:14.........21

Galatians
5:23.........117

Ephesians
1:23.........50
4:32.........104
5.............22, 31, 37, 51, 58, 63,
            65, 69, 71, 94, 104,
            105, 112, 135, 137
5:15–21......37, 38
5:18.........47
5:21.........38, 39, 40, 41, 42, 47,
            54, 93
5:21–24......38

5:22.........38, 39, 43, 47, 49, 54,
            58
5:22–24......47, 48
5:23.........47, 51, 54
5:24.........47, 48, 50, 54
5:25.........43, 64
5:25–33......52, 63, 68
5:26.........64
5:28.........64, 68
5:30.........46
5:31.........93
5:33.........73
6.............43, 104
6:1..........98
6:1–4........93
6:4..........103

Colossians
3:12.........10

1 Timothy
4:3..........17

Titus
2:4..........55
3:3..........116

Philemon
1:1–2........120

Hebrews
13:2.........120
13:4.........17, 112
13:17........43

1 Peter
2............75, 139
2:18–25......82
2:20–21......91
2:22–23......76
3............47, 93, 140

SCRIPTURE INDEX

3:1............76
3:1–2........77
3:1–6........52, 82, 87
3:1–7.........75
3:2...........77, 78

3:3............79
3:3–6........77
3:7...........52, 82, 83, 84, 87, 89,
          139
4:9...........119, 120, 122